Pull the Other One

By the same author:

*Laws and Disorders: A Law-Breaking Guide to Real but
Bizarre Laws From Over the Centuries*
*French Letters & English Overcoats: Sexual Fallacies and
Fads from Ancient Greece to the Millennium*

Pull the Other One

Amazing Real Life Excuses from Around the World

Richard De'ath

 Robson Books

First published in Great Britain in 2000 by Robson Books, 10 Blenheim Court, Brewery Road, London N7 9NT

A member of the Chrysalis Group plc

British Library Cataloguing in Publication Data
A catalogue record for this title is available from the British Library

ISBN 1 86105 349 5

Printed in Great Britain by
Creative Print & Design (Wales), Ebbw Vale, S. Wales

Contents

1

A BAD EXCUSE IS BETTER THAN NONE

'WHAT'S HIS EXCUSE?'

Troilus and Cressida, William Shakespeare (1564–1616)

Stephen Gosson was a sixteenth-century poet, actor, clergyman, pamphleteer and master of the excuse. He never claimed to be one of the founding fathers of the tradition – that honour surely belongs to Adam, whose awakening sexual interest in the Garden of Eden is described in (among many other sources) the monk Robert of Brunne's book, *Handlying Synne*, written in 1303, and sometimes referred to as the earliest manual of advice on talking your way out of trouble, wherein appear the lines, 'He [Adam] wulde haue excusede hys fame, As who sey, "God was to blame."' What Gosson *did* create was the artful practice's most famous expression: 'A bad excuse is better, they say, than none at all.'

Familiar as the shortened version of this line undoubtedly now is, the man to whom we owe a nod of acknowledgement every time we practise what he preached is something of an enigma. He was born, it is believed, in Kent about 1555, became a scholar at Oxford, where he spent most of his time idling or writing poetry, before dropping out at the age of 21 in 1576. His excuse – the first of many he told – was that he wanted to go to London, 'So I shoulde not wither in ye countrie for want of sappe.'

In the capital city, Gosson joined a company of wandering actors and dramatists, dividing his time between appearing in the first public theatres which had recently been built in Shoreditch and Blackfriars, and writing several plays, including a comedy, *Captain Mario*, a drama, *Catilin's Conspiracies*, and a morality tale, *Praise at Parting*. No copies have survived of these works and the evidence suggests he was not a very good actor, either. Then, in 1578, Gosson decided he had had enough of the 'sappe of London' and got himself appointed to the position of parson at Great Wigborough, an isolated parish on the Essex coast near Mersea Island. How he managed this is not known – one of his critics, the wild and rollicking dramatist, Thomas Lodge, who had been a fellow student at Oxford, later taunted him, 'I should blush from a Player to become an enuinouse Preacher' – but the excuse Gosson gave to the local people must have convinced them that here was a reformed sinner with a message: 'I could purge myselfe of slaunder in many words and inveigh against Playes and also bestow my time in teaching young Gentlemen.'

Gosson's life in Great Wigborough was certainly a far cry from the temptations and vagaries of London. He preached in the imposing St Stephen's Church, with its castellated Norman tower, and lived in the adjoining rectory which had fine views out to the coast – both of which still stand today. He also set about biting the hand that had once fed him by writing pamphlets attacking the theatre and 'those Poets, Pipers, Players and such like Caterpillars of the Commonwealth and their mischievous exercises'. In 1579, Gosson published *The School of Abuse*, in which he furiously denounced the performing of plays on the Sabbath. The newly-made parson also accused those who sought to justify such performances with his now-famous satirical line, that a bad excuse (which in this context they *all* were) was better than none at all.

A few years later – and at about the same time as a certain young Will Shakespeare was abroad in London – Gosson turned his attention from the stage to the fair sex and wrote another pamphlet, *Pleasant Quippes for Upstart Newfangled Gentlewomen*, which he published in 1595. Whether or not the bard from Stratford ever cast *his* eye over Gosson's self-important verses, Will's sense of humour would no doubt have been tickled by the sub-title, 'A Plesant Invective Against the Fantastical Forreigne Toyes Dayly Used in Woman's Apparel'. The author once again inserted his excuse for writing the work:

> *But Husbands, you marke well my sawes:*
>   *when they pretend their gentle blood,*
> *Then they intend to make you dawes*
>   *in vaine to spend your wealth and goods.*
> *You better were the clown to cloath,*
> *Than gentles which doe vertue loath.*

Gosson was certainly not the first man to complain about the extravagance of women – nor did he come up with the first excuse to try and stop their expensive ways. But he did stamp his name on the tradition, and it is a shame that it is not better known. It seems that at the turn of the new century, he returned once more to

London and became the Rector of St Botolph's in Bishopsgate. Here he wrote some more poems and pamphlets, attacking the theatre on moral, political and religious grounds. Stephen Gosson died in February 1623, 'on the thirteenthe of the month and was buried in the nighte.' Make what you will of that!

Shakespeare, whose reputation was then very much in the ascendency, might almost have intended the title of one of his earliest plays, *The Comedy of Errors*, to be a sly dig at people like Gosson – certainly Will got in a telling line about excuses, 'She will well excuse, Why at this time the dores are made against you.' He also had his characters use excuses in a number of the other plays including *A Midsummer Night's Dream* ('Stay gentle Helena, heare my excuse'), *Henry IV* ('My nephewes trespasse . . . hath the excuse of youth') and *Two Gentlemen of Verona* ('To morrow be in readiness to go, excuse it not for I am peremptory').

Writers had, of course, been recording the history of excusing since long before the time of Shakespeare. Apart from the aforementioned English monk, Robert of Brunne, scholars in France and Germany had discussed the topic at least two centuries earlier and, in 1494, the rules of the English guilds decreed that, 'Noo man then be absent withoute a resonable and sufficiaunt excuse.' (Today's employers might like to note that nothing changes!) A couple of hundred years later, Thomas Hobbes wrote in his masterpiece of political philosophy, *Leviathan* (1651), 'To accuse requires less eloquence than to excuse,' while at the end of the century, the *Dictionary of Cant* (1700) devoted a whole section to the 'Lame Excuse, a sorry Shift or Evasion'.

Novelists, too, reflected this element of everyday life in their narratives: Richard Brinsley Sheridan in his tale of *Sidney Biddulph* (1761) put familiar words into the mouth of one of his characters, 'I am weary of inventing excuses from absenting myself.' The well-known American author, Harriet Beecher Stowe, and England's Mary Russell Mitford were also responsible for portraits of people we could all identify: in Stowe's *Uncle Tom's Cabin* (1850) it is, 'Dinah, the mistress of the whole art and mystery of excuse making,' while in Mitford's *Our Village* (1834) we learn, 'She was the excuser-general of the neighbourhood, turning every speech and action the sunny side without.'

The excuse, *per se*, hardly needs defining. Some dictionaries refer to it simply as 'freeing from blame or guilt', but the *Oxford English Dictionary* is rather more specific and actually sets out the credo that I have adopted in making my selection of humorous stories for this book: 'that which is offered as a reason for being excused; sometimes in a bad sense, a mere pretext, a subterfuge.' Excuses are, of course, met in all aspects of life: at home, at work, at play, in the making (and breaking) of marriages, in social engagements (ditto), in travelling, in dealing with bureaucracy and, particularly, when encountering the laws of the land. Indeed, it has sometimes seemed to me that the word 'excuse' should really be spelt with an 'i' because excuses are all a mixture of invention, ingenuity and inspiration. Someone once said, 'Two wrongs don't make a right' – but to that could be added, 'but they *do* make a good excuse!'

Neither the publishers nor I have the excuse to make you buy this book, that it is the first of its kind. Over the years, there have been quite a number of volumes proffering guidance on *how* to make excuses and *when* to use them, as well as offering pages of suggestions for *every* situation. *Pull the Other One* is, though, different to the others in that every example herein is *true*. Only the names and the places have been changed in certain instances to protect the *really* embarrassed.

There are, of course, some stories which I have collected during my research that I'd like to believe are true, although the details are scant. Particularly scanty (if you'll excuse the pun) are the stories of adultery. Especially ones like that of the angry husband from a London suburb who discovered his wife in bed with another man. 'What the hell are you doing?' the man shouted. 'See,' the wife said to the lover, 'I told you he was stupid.' Then there was the New York housewife, also caught *inflagrento delecto* across silken sheets with an equally naked man, who teased her furious spouse standing in the bedroom doorway, 'You always have a good excuse for coming home *late*, Bill, now let's hear you come up with a good one for being *early!*'

More intriguing still is the story about the Queen on a trip to an African country. She was being driven in a horse-drawn carriage when one of the animals suddenly let off a huge fart. 'I'm so sorry,' the Queen whispered to the leader of the nation sitting beside her. 'Oh, don't worry,' legend has it the man replied, 'if you hadn't said anything, I'd have thought it was the horse!'

Recently, a group of researchers at Brigham Young University in America – the seat of learning named after the leader of the Mormons – conducted an enquiry into the use of lies and excuses on television programmes. The results of their research pointed to the fact that more lies were told in soap operas than any other type of programme. A spokesman of the university was quoted in *The New York Times* in March 2000:

Our study revealed that these shows featured five lies an

hour – most by women to men. But what shocked us most was that none of the characters worried about lying!

One man who loved a good excuse was Samuel Butler, the nineteenth-century author best remembered for his autobiographical novel, *The Way of All Flesh* (1903) and the Utopian satire published in 1872, *Erewhon* – the title is an inversion of nowhere – in which many conventional practices are reversed. Crime, for example, is treated as an illness and illness a crime, while machines have been banned for fear of them gaining mastery over the minds of men and women. (Now *there's* a thought!) An expression Butler used in the course of the book reads like this: 'Any fool can tell the truth, but it requires a man of some sense to know how to tell a lie well.'

If you add women to that and substitute the word 'excuse' for 'lie', then you have a pretty good idea of what is to be found in the pages that follow. And if some of the stories don't make you laugh, then just blame Stephen Gosson who put it all in perspective!

2

PUBLIC INCONVENIENCES

A few years ago a journalist on *The Birmingham Post* was writing a story about yet another chapter of delays on the railways, for which British Rail could offer only the most feeble excuses. After cataloguing the cancellations, interruptions and late arrivals of the services to and from the nation's second city, the writer concluded wearily: 'There is apparently very little fear on the part of the travelling public that their inconveniences will be seriously interfered with.'

The fact of the matter is that when it comes to excuses and the making of excuses, British Rail has been way ahead of all the other public services for years. From the now legendary claims that delays to trains have been caused by, alternately, 'leaves on the line' or 'the wrong kind of snow', the railway system has consistently beaten off all challengers in the excuses department. There was not even much comfort for hard-pressed commuters when Chris Leah, the director of operations for Railtrack, agreed in *The Times* in November 1999 that although for years leaves had been the butt of railway jokes, they were still a serious problem and added:

'But Britain is now the world leader in dealing with them.'

ONE MORE BRIDGE TO CROSS

Excuses for train delays go back almost to the birth of the railways. One of the earliest is also one of the best and was described in a historical feature about the advent of the railroad in America. The story, told in the *Kansas City Star*, described the building of the track between St Louis and Jefferson City, Missouri, in 1855. The inaugural run was set for November in that year and a group of 200 specially invited passengers were waved off from St Louis. When the train failed to arrive, however, red-faced officials of the new line had to proffer an almost unbelievable excuse to the press:

Regretfully, the company must inform its patrons that owing to an oversight by our engineers the rail tracks connecting the two ends of a bridge over the Gasconade River had not been connected.

SNOWED UNDER

In Britain, it was bad weather rather than unconnected bridges that caused the operators some of their earliest problems. Snow was a particular headache in the more outlying districts. In December 1902, the *Cambridge News* carried this item from an official source, which just goes to show that very little has changed in the intervening century:

British Rail have stated that they are fully prepared this year if the snow catches them unawares.

HOT NEWS

For years the *ABC Railway Guide*, which was first published in 1874, attempted to provide travellers with details of services across the length and breadth of the British Isles. Many a complaint was no doubt made based on the information printed in all good faith in the pages of the annual publication. But just occasionally, examples of humour crept into the *Guide*, as in this statement published in 1953:

British Rail have said that it is hoped from January 1 a normal service will run to the West Country with trains liable to delays of up to 20 minutes.

BEHIND THE ONE IN FRONT

In 1963, *The Railway Gazette* ran a Christmas competition to find the best excuse given by a railway employee in explanation of a delayed or cancelled train. The first prize was awarded to this statement by a British Rail guard, which was noted down and sent in by a traveller on the Euston line:

We apologise for the late running of this train. This is due to us following a train that is in front of us.

CONSERVING ENERGY

There was some confusion on the platform at Hamble railway station near Southampton in January 1965 when a train for Portsmouth pulled up and an announcement was heard repeating: 'Passengers are not to board this train which has only stopped here to let you know that it does not stop here on Sundays.' The group of stranded travellers were then forced to walk to the next station, Netley, to catch a train, and on arrival at Portsmouth lodged a complaint with British Rail as well as informing the local paper, the *Southern Evening Echo*. A reporter asked BR for an explanation and a spokesman responded:

This is an economy measure. We save the power it takes to stop a train as well as the power it takes to start one. Braking must become cost-effective.

THE NAKED PASSENGER

The case of Walter Harris who was arrested on another Portsmouth train going to London in April 1970 made headlines in the national press because he was *stark naked* at the time. According to the subsequent court case at Old Street Magistrates Court reported in the *News of the World*, when Harris was questioned by a Detective Sergeant Nichols about his state of undress he replied:

Everybody has his own peculiarities; this is mine. I have been travelling naked in trains for about two years, but I did not think anyone had seen me.

THE BARE FACTS – AGAIN

Not one but *three* naked men were reported sitting in a carriage of a Dublin to Cork train a decade later, according to a story in *The Irish Times* in May 1982. The trio were reported by a group of school girls to a ticket collector, John O'Callaghan, who went to investigate and found all three without a stitch on. One of the men told O'Callaghan:

A man that none of us had ever met before got on the train and invited us to join in a game of strip poker. He won all our clothes and then got off the train at the last stop.

JUST THE TICKET!

Explaining some new regulations that had been introduced by British Rail in December 1978 to come into effect the following year, a spokesman was asked about the dangers of terrorist acts on the railways. Mr Colin Herbert, speaking for BR, told *The Observer:*

Would-be saboteurs have a perfect right to be on a platform provided they have bought a ticket. It is not the job of our staff to arrest passengers carrying rocket-launchers. If a passenger with a genuine ticket is seen to be carrying a launcher, or an atomic bomb for that matter, our staff have orders to notify the proper authorities and to exercise common sense while awaiting developments.

TAKES THE SANDWICH

Harold Watson of Derby, who described himself as a 'professional philosopher', told a story that was a bit hard to swallow when he was charged in December 1980 with travelling without a valid ticket and also trespassing on railway property. According to a report in the *Derby Evening Telegraph*, when Watson was brought before the local magistrates court he asked for 'about 5000' other offences to be taken into consideration. He explained to the bench:

I have been living off stolen railway sandwiches – and only off stolen railway sandwiches – for the last fifteen years.

THE ARMCHAIR TRAVELLER

When train services to and from Liverpool were disrupted one day in October 1979, another spokesman for British Rail offered a curious double excuse to angry passengers and the press. The *Liverpool Echo* carried the following statement:

First a train from Ormskirk to Liverpool struck an armchair at Kirkdale, Lancashire. Later a train from Liverpool hit a pram at almost the same spot.

THE BIG MOUSETAKE

When British Rail's West Coast Way was suddenly closed down on 17 November 1983, staff as well as passengers were left annoyed and bewildered – all the more so when the cause of the disruption was attributed to a *mouse*. The events were reported the following day by the *Daily Mirror*, which said the drama had begun when signalman Trevor Hockam 'was chased around the lever room of his box for four hours by a white mouse'. Unable to get rid of the creature, Hockam had closed down the line and walked 16 miles along the track to Bognor Regis before heading for his home in Littlehampton. His wife later explained to the press:

Trevor is not frightened of animals. In fact, he is very fond of them. We used to have two goldfish.

TREADING A FINE LINE

Passengers on a high-speed intercity train running between Birmingham and London in October 1983 were suddenly amazed to catch sight of a figure scrambling along the roof of the carriages. The guard was called and subsequently managed to arrest the sure-footed Glenn Massey, according to a report in the *Birmingham Mail*. When asked to explain his behaviour, Massey, who was later sentenced to 200 hours of community service for his pains, excused himself:

I was in possession of a second-class ticket and I was looking for the bar.

THE WRONG TRAIN

Even the chairman of British Rail has been known to suffer the foibles of his service. In July 1987, the then chairman, Sir Peter Parker, was scheduled to address a meeting of Cumbria County Council in Carlisle. On his way to the assembly in a car, he was delayed by heavy traffic and arrived at Crewe Station to see that a train was just about to leave the platform. Waving his BR pass at the ticket inspector, Sir Peter flung open a carriage door and leaped on to the departing train. For a while, the chairman sat in his seat congratulating himself on having caught the train – until he suddenly realised from the station signs hurtling by that he was not on an express to Carlisle but a non-stop service to London! Appreciating he would never get to the meeting on time, he managed to persuade a guard to throw a note out of the window of the train as it passed through Tamworth Station in Staffordshire. The message read, 'Please apologise to Cumbria Council and tell them I won't be at the meeting on time.' Sir Peter then made plans once he got back to London to *fly* to Cumbria. Explaining his adventure later, he told *The Daily Telegraph*:

It just goes to show that it can happen to anyone.

CROW HALT

It would be wrong, of course, to imagine that it is only British railways that cock things up and then have to come up with excuses. There are examples of the same kind of thing all over the world and here are just a few examples from recent years. In Japan, in November 1986, the fame of the legendary 'bullet train' was dented when two of the super-fast, long-distance trains were stopped dead in their tracks. An embarrassed official of the national rail service in Tokyo told the *Reuter's News Agency*:

The trains were halted because a crow caused a short circuit in the system.

POSTED ABROAD

There were equally red faces the following year in Australia, when the police department of the national network issued a poster which they believed showed a typical fare dodger approaching a station barrier at Calvary Station in Canberra. But, according to a report in the *Canberra Times*, the man in the photograph was actually Mr Dennis Clyne, the Mayor of Calvary. A spokesman of the Australian Rail Police owned up:

We asked an advertising agency for a suitable photograph.

We thought it gave the right impression and when I rang them up to check that it was usable, they said that the man was an undischarged bankrupt who had left the country, so we went ahead.

DINING FOR FREE

The cheek of a penniless bank clerk in Jordan, Majob Khouri, made international news in July 1988 and was reported in several British papers including the *Daily Express*. Khouri tried to get a free meal in a train buffet car travelling to Amman by claiming to be the secretary of the railway director. At this, a waiter pointed out that the director was actually *in* the dining car – but to the clerk's surprise the man confirmed that he was, in fact, his secretary. The *Express* continued:

Later, Khouri apologised for the pretence. The man smiled, saying: 'Do you really think I'm the railway director?'

SPITTING OUT THE TRUTH

Spitting in railway stations has long been a problem in India. Despite the provision of spittoons and the threat of criminal proceedings, little has changed said a report in the *Bombay Times*. In the summer of 1999, however, a special squad was sent into the main railway station in Bombay to try and stop commuters who repeatedly spat wherever they liked. One defiant traveller summarised the feelings of many:

It's just an excuse by the railways to save cleaning costs. I will spit as and when I like – and anywhere I feel.

THE FESTIVE SPIRIT?

Travellers in France hold the national system, SNCF, in rather higher regard than British Rail, but the service can also come up with some pretty good excuses. In December 1999, a passenger journeying between Rouen and Paris wrote to *Paris Match* to describe the explanation he was given when buying a ticket:

I purchased my usual off-peak ticket and enquired why it was dearer than normal. I was told, 'Because it is Christmas.'

A TALE OF YORKSHIRE GRIT

Two new factors have recently been added to the litany of railway excuses. In November 1998, Eurotunnel, the operators of the Channel Tunnel freight and passenger trains, blamed massive disruption to their services on 'the wrong kind of wind', according to a report in *The Mail on Sunday*. A year later, in September 1999, trains running on the 15-mile Wharfedale line in Yorkshire between Ilkley and Leeds were subjected to a new menace. A spokesman for Northern Spirit, which runs the line, explained to *The Daily Telegraph*:

Passengers have complained that they cannot see out of the windows and have missed their stations in the dark. We have investigated the cause of this blackout because we are used to dealing with normal muck. But this is the wrong kind of dirt caused by dust from the brake blocks on our trains.

THERE WILL BE A SHORT DELAY

But not even leaves, snow, wind or dirt could be used to

excuse the delay to passengers on a train between Middlesbrough and Hartlepool on Teesside on 3 December 1999. Once again, it was an employee of Northern Spirit who had to explain to commuters boarding the train why it would be 15 minutes leaving the station. *The Times* was just one of several papers to carry the explanation which one passenger described as 'the most ridiculous thing I've ever heard':

The service is delayed today because the driver is only five feet one inches tall and his swivel chair has broken. He is too short to reach the pedals.

THE TOP TEN EXCUSES

The monthly magazine for rail enthusiasts, *Railway World*, rounded off the twentieth century with a listing of British Rail's most unlikely excuses for delays to its services. The top ten, not in any particular order, were these:

- *The guard has been left behind by accident.*
- *There is a man with an umbrella on the line.*
- *A rat has bitten through a power cable.*
- *The rails are slippery.*
- *There are high tides at Portsmouth Harbour.*
- *A horse is on the track.*
- *Ammonia from an ice rink has leaked on the line.*
- *There are some pigs in our way.*
- *A lunatic has climbed over a fence near the station.*
- *Fighting has broken out among the passengers.*

THE PROBLEMS OF COMMUNICATION

British Telecom also has quite a reputation for trotting out comic excuses. In 1973, a reader of *The Times* in the Midlands wrote to the paper's famous letters page about a communication he had received from his local BT head of operations. It informed the man that he was now connected to the STD network and continued:

Would you please try your telephone now, and if you are unable to use it would you please report the difficulty by dialling 151. Please let me know if you do not receive this letter.

A CUTTING MOMENT

When the old telephone exchange at Ruislip in Middlesex was due to give way to a new £1.8 million exchange in January 1982, it was decided to cut off every existing line just before the new system came into services. To achieve this, said a report in the *Middlesex Advertiser and Gazette*, BT engineers decided to loop string through 9,000 plugs and provide 20 men to pull on the string at exactly the same moment. To make something of a ceremony of the event, the Mayor of Ruislip was invited to give the command to pull the string at 1.30 pm on 'Changeover Day'. Commenting on the subsequent events, a Telecom spokesman said:

Several thousand people were, of course, cut off. But all subscribers had been sent letters warning them that a momentary shut-down was likely to occur.

BLANKED OUT

An official from British Telecom in his TV detection van became increasingly puzzled in December 1981 as he searched for the residents of Lower and Middle Hambledon in Rutland who, according to his list, had not paid their television licences. Finally, an account of the event in the *Stamford News* said, the man stopped policeman PC James Sutherland as he was cycling by. The officer later explained to the newspaper:

He told me he was trying to find out why the residents had not renewed their licences. I said they would be difficult to contact as the villages had both been submerged beneath Rutland Reservoir in 1974.

DIAL 'W' FOR WARMTH . . .

The frustration caused by finding telephone boxes out of order or not working is familiar enough. But few better excuses have been offered than that given in 1988 by an operator in Kidderminster when she was contacted by a local man, Walter Station. After finding that the phone near his home was not working, Station used a neighbour's phone to call the operator. He relayed the information he was given to the *Daily Mail*:

She told me condensation was the cause of the trouble. But the phone would work perfectly well if I warmed the handset under my armpit.

. . . OR 'M' FOR MUDDLE

Christopher Logue, the *Private Eye* columnist, is a great

collector of trifles about the misfortunes of the communications industry. One of his favourite stories was a quote from *The Daily Telegraph* of November 1979, which stated:

A spokesman for the Post Office said, 'We apologise for the inconvenience, but more than five million homes without telephones are to get letters from us explaining why their bills have been delayed.'

STANDING ORDERS

Humour is not normally to be found in the wordy pages of the *Amendments to the Post Office Guide*. But in the July 1966 edition, staff who received a copy must have enjoyed the extract which referred to 'Page 47 – Prohibitions', for underneath was the amendment undoubtedly intended to avoid any misunderstanding:

Line 1. After *Contraceptives;* insert *fresh meat and other food-stuffs.*

KEEP THE POSTCODES CLEAN

When the Post Office decided to introduce postcodes in the 1970s, a long list was circulated to all relevant departments of the organisation with instructions on those letters it was permissible to use and those which should be avoided. According to a spokesman quoted in the *Hampstead and Highgate Express* in April 1973:

Although we do not wish to appear to be too rigid in this matter, BF and BO are not to be used in any area.

BETTER THAN HIS BITE

Stories of postmen being attacked by dogs are a popular source of comedians' jokes and the painful experience of rather too many GPO employees. In a case in Bedford in 1978, postman Bob Mills killed a large Alsatian which attacked him while he was delivering mail. Mills had seized a fork that was leaning against a wall and speared the animal. The enraged owner later took the postman to court, according to a report in the *Bedfordshire Times*, where Mills was asked why he did not come at the dog with the other end of the fork to avoid killing him. The postman replied:

Well, why didn't he come at me with the other end?

POSTED SAFELY

The *Yorkshire Post* reported in June 1985 that GPO officials in Sheffield were trying to make contact with a Mr Sarab Ali who had apparently been posting £1 notes in post boxes. A spokesman said that Ali had already signed and inserted over a thousand £1 notes into a number of boxes across the city, and added:

Mr Ali is not an idiot. To use pillar boxes as piggy-banks merely denotes a profound misunderstanding of our savings system.

THE MESSAGE IS (UN)CLEAR?

The Australian public servants who boobed over that railway poster of the mayor as a fare dodger had no better excuse than the officials of the Australian Post

Office who similarly withdrew a poster in November 1984. According to *The Sydney Morning Herald* they decided against displaying a picture which showed the American and Russian leaders, Reagan and Chernenko, smiling over two Christmas cards they had sent each other. The reason for the ban?

The poster lacks a clear message.

LETTER OF THE LAW

The case of a Nottingham postman, Paul Woolley, who was sacked for not attending an interview with a company doctor, made the newspapers in December 1999. Woolley took his case for unfair dismissal to an employment tribunal where he sought compensation and reinstatement after being penalised for taking time off for stress, which he claimed had been caused by managers bullying him. Reporting the case, *The Times* added:

The postman, who it was ruled was unfairly dismissed for missing the urgent appointment, may get his job back after it was discovered that a letter from his Royal Mail bosses alerting him to the meeting had been lost in the post.

COOKED TO PERFECTION

The Gas Board has had its fair share of tricky situations to explain – but there have been few more amusing than the case of the Norfolk man found sitting in an armchair on top of a gas holder one Sunday morning in May 1954. According to an account in the *East Anglian Daily Times*, the man, Albert Miller, was an employee of the company and said he regularly sat on top of the huge structure. A Gas Board spokesman reported his excuse:

I take my armchair up there every Sunday when the weather is fine to read the Sunday paper. My weight gives just the extra pressure needed to cook the dinners.

THE ANSWER LIES IN THE EATING

A Bedfordshire housewife Mrs Jimson of Olney had no such help with her gas cooker. In fact, after eight visits from test fitters sent by the local Gas Board, the gas flow on her new appliance was still uneven. As a result of this – an account of the events in the *Daily Express* of July 1967 stated – a Gas Board cook was actually sent to Olney to do a test bake. According to Mrs Jimson, the sponge mix came out of her oven 'looking like lumpy custard'. A British Gas Corporation spokeswoman, however, put quite a different spin on things:

The sponge was delicious. Greatly superior to another sponge baked from the same mix in our show-room demonstration.

THE CANARY IS DEAD!

A canary found dead in its cage after a visit by Gas Board fitters in Barnet in February 1977 gave rise to an extraordinary admission from an official of the company. Mrs Jane Weaver left the bird in his cage in her flat while some gas pipes were being cleaned. Although on her return the bird seemed unusually quiet, it was not until the following morning that Mrs Weaver realised her little pet was dead and had been fixed in an upright position with Sellotape. She angrily rang the Gas Board – an account in *The People* stated – to demand an explanation. A spokesman for the Board told the newspaper:

We are going to supply our customer with a new canary. We have an arrangement with a bird dealer who supplies us with about 200 birds a year. Normally we just pop a ringer in the cage and say no more about it. However, on this occasion the engineers got through their work on the pipes in record time and Mrs Weaver was allowed home before we could effect a replacement.

WHAT A SPECTACLE!

It was cows rather than canaries which featured in another classic Gas Board excuse on the other side of the world in New Zealand in 1967. During the spring of that year, farmers in the Taranaki District on North Island reported that a new disease seemed to have struck their cattle because they were all going blind. An enquiry revealed that the cause was probably a new natural gas pipeline which was being laid by welders between Kapuni and the coast. A spokesman for the gas company told the *Wellington Evening Post*:

Nobody had explained to the cows that it's dangerous to watch a welder at work unless you wear dark glasses. Now we are going to fit them with pairs specially designed for cows.

AN EXPLOSIVE EXCUSE

Gas bills sent out to customers which are based on

estimates have been a source of disagreement between the Gas Board and the public for many years. But probably the most extraordinary instance of this was the case of Arthur Purdy of Rochdale, who was so incensed by the estimate he received in October 1986 that he complained to Northern Gas as well as informing the *Rochdale Observer* about the special circumstances behind the bill. A spokesman thereupon released this statement:

We agree it was rather high for this time of year. We think that Mr Purdy may have been charged for the gas used up during the explosion that blew his house to pieces.

SHOCKING FACTS – 1

Like the Gas Board, the various electricity companies through the UK have made their contributions to the lore of excuses over the years. Back in the 1940s, a sign board posted beside a number of power lines in the south-east of England had to be taken down – with apologies – when its ludicrous statement was pointed out to the CGEB:

BEWARE!
To touch these wires is instant death
Anyone found doing so will be prosecuted

SHOCKING FACTS – 2

Ed O'Rourke of Tampa Bay, Florida, took quite the opposite view when he ignored just such a warning in January 2000. After climbing on to an electricity transformer and being thrown 40 feet and electrocuted by 13,000 volts from which he was lucky to survive, O'Rourke said he was going to sue the electricity company. The excuse he gave to the *Jacksonville Journal* in Florida was this:

I am suing the company for failing to prevent me from gaining access to a fenced, locked and gated electricity sub-station. I am also suing six bars who sold me alcohol and caused me to climb the transformer in a drunken stupor.

A CANINE INCONVENIENCE

It is not only humans that need to be kept away from electricity lines. In October 1964, the *Sheffield Telegraph* in Yorkshire reported the sudden fall of a power line which had been caused by the collapse of a metal support. It had fallen across one of the city's busiest streets much used by dog walkers on their way to a nearby park. A spokesman of the electricity company told the *Telegraph*:

I blame the animal-lovers. The standard's base was all corroded.

SUPPORTING CURRENTS

The Zambian Electricity Board also faced a problem with its pylons in the spring of 1988. Following a series of power cuts, engineers were instructed to carry out an investigation and report back to company headquarters. The general administrator of the board, Essie Mulonda, then offered this excuse to the local paper, *News From Zambia*, on June 8:

*The main cause of the power cuts in our country is not the
inefficiency of our engineers, but the thieves who take the
crossbars from our pylons and turn them into bed frames.*

IN DEEP TROUBLE

The water authorities are equally culpable of excuse-
making. In the spring of 1986, the Lancashire Water
Authority announced that it was removing all the fish
from a popular angling spot known as Lytham Pond. In
April, a spokesman was questioned about the decision
by a correspondent of the *Angler's Mail* and said:

*The pond is actually situated in an abandoned cemetery.
I admit that several double-figure carp have been landed by
local anglers, but we have received numerous letters pointing
out that the site was never intended to give pleasure to people.
Furthermore, the proprietors of St Anne's Crematorium,
which is only a few yards from the pond, say that their
services for the dead are being upset by the smell of the
anglers' fry-ups.*

THE HOLE TRUTH?

The unexpected collapse of a 400-yard section of the
new Carsington Reservoir Dam, not far from Matlock
in Derbyshire, in June 1984 caused consternation to the
local water authority as well as the consulting engineers
who had built it. A spokesman for the two organisations
told the *Derbyshire Times* that a full enquiry was being
conducted, and added:

*We are looking for something, but it is difficult to say what
we are looking for until we find it. When we come across it,*

we will know what it is. But if we knew what we were looking for, we would not be looking.

THE SMELL OF THE BRINY

In July 1980, the *Sussex Express* reported that 'several hundred' bathers had complained about the bad smell of the sea at Camber on the coast near Hastings. Suggestions that this might have been caused by sewage going into the sea were dismissed by an official of the Channel Water Service, Joshua Robinson, who was quoted by the *Express* giving an aside about the holiday-makers:

What do they know about it? The sea always smells bad at this time of year. It's nature.

RAIN CHECK

And, finally, a writer to *The Times* in April 2000 raised the perennial question as to whether all the country's reservoirs were full and if the regular plea to conserve water would be issued. The letter from Roger Ordish of East Sussex, added:

I am expecting any day now to hear that the answer is 'No' and that it was the wrong kind of rain . . .

3

BUREAUCRATIC
BOOBS

Bureaucrats are among the masters of the great excuse – those fulsome ranks of men and women who fill every position from humble council official to government minister. It is one of the facts of life that those put in authority (*any* authority) have to become adept at side-stepping awkward questions from the press, the public and even, on occasions, their own colleagues. Not surprisingly, quite a few of them have made the proverbial pig's ear of trying to set the record straight as this chapter will all too comically demonstrate.

Politics is especially rich in examples of obfuscations, fibs and excuses in general, and Britain's Deputy Prime Minister, the garrulous John Prescott, has proved himself something of a champion of the tradition. In March 2000, for example, he was interviewed about his plans for house building by Nick Robinson of BBC Television's *News 24*. Confusing himself with the distinction between 'single parents' and 'single-occupancy', the ebullient politician suddenly stopped and said, 'That's crap. I can do better than that. Can we do it again?' To which Robinson replied, quietly, 'Deputy Prime Minister, don't you realise we are live?'

In an earlier interview in October 1999 with BBC Radio's John Humphreys, Prescott was challenged that in the past he had called for transport ministers to resign when accidents had occurred, and that members of the public were entitled to demand that someone at the top should carry the blame. The minister replied:

If it's the man at the top – there are far too many responsible for these matters. I'm not entirely responsible. I am responsible to try and get a safer railway, but it's not like it's publicly owned, where I could send an edict out to the chairman and say I want it done ABC.

However, John Prescott's classic for *Pull the Other One* was uttered during the Labour Party Conference at Brighton. When asked by reporters why he chose to use one of his pair of official Jaguar cars for a journey of less than 300 yards from his hotel to the conference centre, Prescott – nick-named Two Jags as a result – spluttered,

'My wife doesn't like to have her hair blown about.'

WHEELY GOOD EXCUSE

John Prescott apart, the Houses of Parliament are a prime spot to hear ministers proffering excuses all the time. One example in January 2000 is already acknowledged as unique among its kind. The questioner was Labour MP, Tom Cox, who enquired of the Transport Department, 'Who will regulate nifty and often dangerous jet skis?' The reply, proffered by the Minister, Keith Hill, and recorded in the pages of *Hansard*, stated:

The total length of the London Cycle Network route is some 755 miles.

RIDDEN TO A STANDSTILL

Bicycles also featured in another excuse offered in 1989 by an official of the Royal Society for the Prevention of Accidents (ROSPA). According to a report in *The Observer*, the famous cycling proficiency test taken by generations of riders was to be replaced by a new road safety scheme. Commenting on this, ROSPA's education officer, John Richardson, explained to one of the paper's reporters:

The proficiency test has become rather pedestrian.

NO TIME FOR A JOB

In the decade after the Second World War, the Ministry of Labour issued a great many bewildering forms to those seeking employment. It was not surprising that members of the public were often confused by the instructions, but sometimes even the bureaucrats befuddled themselves and needed to send letters of excuse like this one headed, 'Note to Employer' which was reprinted in the *Daily Mirror* in 1953:

It is regretted that it was not possible to send the enclosed forms to you before the date by which, had you received them in time, you would be required to forward completed copies to the local Employment Exchange.

A FACT OF DEATH

'Anything the Brits can do we can do better' might have been the motto of the civil servants working for the US Government during the 1950s. In 1954, *The New York*

Times ran an article highlighting official lunacy in the workplace and cited the following as one of the best its reporters had spotted. It was taken from a Government Order on 'Leave Regulations' and stated under Section 3:

When an employee absent from duty on account of illness dies without making application for advanced sick leave, the fact of death is sufficient to show a 'serious disability' and to dispense with the requirement of a formal application and a medical certificate.

THE SERIOUS PROBLEM OF HOLES

Another government official, who – perhaps wisely – remained anonymous, was asked in 1971 for a statement about the administration's attitude towards medical care by the editor of the *American Journal of Public Health*. During the course of his diatribe, which defended the Government's record on health, the spokesman stated:

One on the outside who criticises the placement of square pegs in round holes should be sure that there are not more round holes and square pegs than there are square holes and round pegs. Even if this is not the case, the critic should be certain that round holes are not a more serious problem than square ones, and he should withhold his criticism unless he is quite sure that it is better to leave round holes unfilled than it is to fill them partially with square pegs.

ASK A SILLY QUESTION . . .

When Terry Burrows, the works manager of a yarn-spinning mill in Carlisle, received a curious request from his local Department of Social Security in 1970, his sense of humour got the better of him. The enquiry was in conjunction with an injury claim by an employee who had damaged his foot while taking a short cut to work over a wall. The letter from the DSS asked, 'Is it necessary for your employees to climb a six-foot, glass-topped wall to get to work?' The *Daily Mail* got wind of the matter and reprinted Burrows' reply:

The normal mode of entry for employees is by using the springboard provided, bouncing over the mill surround, climbing the outside of Dixon's [285 feet] chimney, and descending inside the chimney and entering the place of work via the boiler house.

'POOR' EXCUSE

Since democracy replaced communism in Russia, the excuse has found a whole new meaning among the people. At a stroke, one of the oldest jokes became defunct: 'The Moscow returning officer had no excuse to offer when he had to announce that next year's election results had been stolen.' However, this tradition did not die with the coming of political freedom. In October 1999, it was announced that Vladimir Zhirinovsky had been given the right to stand in the following December's parliamentary elections – despite determined efforts to stop his candidacy and that of several other members of his right-wing bloc. The objection to the group, according to a report in *Pravda*, was because 'some candidates withheld details about their wealth'. Explaining the reason why they were now being allowed to take part in the elections, Zhirinovsky said:

We will have only poor candidates.

BURIAL WORKS

That there is really nothing new in examples of foot-in-mouth by government ministers may be judged by this example from 1925. It occurred while a leading Conservative front-bench spokesman, William Chambers, was replying to an attack by Labour MPs about his government's road-building plans. He was heard to mutter:

You know, I think they are making the most enormous mole out of a mountain.

THE UNLUCKY VIEW

In August 1934, the officials of Margate Town Council in Kent announced that it had been decided not to use the number '13' for numbering houses in the district. A report of the decision in the *Kent Messenger* described a debate on the issue by members and added:

It was noted that ladies who use numbers '13' bathing machines seldom come out well in a photograph.

WHO'S A NAUGHTY BOY?

An equally comic example of official reasoning was evident in a decision by the British Council in November 1976. The Council ordered that a 10-second sequence from a specially-made educational film about the life of budgerigars should be removed. The offending scene apparently involved two budgerigars in the sex act, a report in the *Daily Express* stated, and a British Council spokesman explained the reason behind their decision:

This could give offence to the citizens of Cairo.

JUST A PONG AT CHRISTMAS

The town of Wisbech in Norfolk has for many years prided itself on its Christmas festivities. These always began with the arrival of Father Christmas, who was introduced by the mayor to the local people assembled in the town square. In 1944, however, things went somewhat awry, as a report in the *Wisbech Standard* reveals:

Introducing the guest of honour, the Mayor explained that the reason Father Christmas had not arrived earlier in the festive season was because the Town Council had inadvertently sent the cesspool emptier to meet him instead of a lorry.

TO BE TAKEN WITH A PINCH OF SALT

The Christmas season also brings transport problems to the people of Montreal in Canada. For years the city authorities tried to find an answer to the heavy snows that always threatened to bring the metropolis to a standstill. In the winter of 1952, the *Montreal Star* quoted an authority spokesman on yet another bureaucratic blunder:

The use of salt for snow clearing after an experiment on Friday was discontinued because (a) the snow was too deep and the weather too cold, and (b) the salt melted instead of vice-versa. So shovel gangs continued to remove in the old-fashioned way.

THE EXPLANATION IS OBVIOUS – 1

After all the problems in the past with prohibition and gangsterism in the state of Illinois, the authorities pride themselves on their dedication to public service. But the *Chicago Sun-Times* in 1955 could not resist running on its front page an announcement which stated:

The State Senate of Illinois has announced that its Committee on Efficiency and Economy is to be disbanded, 'for reasons of efficiency and economy'.

THE EXPLANATION IS OBVIOUS – 2

The same sense of dedication was no doubt behind the decision of the group of High Wycombe councillors when they announced the formation of a new committee in the autumn of 1958. The *Bucks Free Press* informed its readers without a hint of sarcasm:

A Council of Action has been set up. This decided yesterday not to take any immediate action.

GRATE EXPECTATIONS

The news that a layout of metal grids, designed to stop stray sheep from wandering into a housing estate in Ebbw Vale, were to be ripped up and replaced by a new type of grill, was greeted with mixed enthusiasm by the local residents in June 1958. According to a report in *The Daily Telegraph*, the new grills would have narrower bars – the point of which was explained by an Ebbw Vale council official, George Cramp:

Sheep are by no means as silly as is commonly thought.

Several observers have seen them tiptoeing across the existing grids, and on at least two occasions younger sheep have been spotted rolling across the grids, commando-style.

A NOSE FOR TROUBLE

An official with a particularly difficult excuse to proffer to the world was an unnamed employee of the government of the remote Gilbert and Ellice Islands in the Pacific Ocean. In June 1963, it was announced that an inhabitant of Funafuti, one of the Ellice islands, had been charged with biting off his wife's nose. A news bulletin circulated by the government and reprinted in the *Sunday Express* quoted the official as stating:

This custom originated with the coming of the British flag.

GUN LAW

The use of firearms in America has become an increasingly controversial issue in recent years. Back in 1964, the lawmakers in the state of Nebraska, obviously acting with the very best of intentions, agreed upon a new ordinance – but ended up desperately looking for an excuse when it was published because the precise wording read:

No person shall discharge or cause to be discharged any firearm or other lethal weapon on or within sixty feet of any State Highway, except with intent to destroy some noxious animal, or an officer of the Police in the performance of his duty.

IT NEVER RAINS . . .

During one of the wettest months on record at Wetherall near Manchester in June 1968, complaints were made to the local council by several members of the public about a group of workmen watering flowers in the midst of a storm. The men were all wearing waterproof clothing to protect themselves from the downpour and were seen hosing a dozen flower tubs near the town centre. Later they moved on to another location and continued the same activity. A report in the *Manchester Evening News* quoted a council spokesman's response to the complaints:

As is well known, the weather in this part of the country is unreliable. We feel we cannot rely on the rain to feed and reach the roots of public plants.

. . . BUT IT POURS

Bad weather put another member of officialdom in an embarrassing spot in March 1979. He was the spokesman for NATO who had to relay to journalists the reason why 'Operation White Fox' had just been cancelled. This was to be an exercise 'to test the readiness of NATO's frontline alpine commandos under adverse weather conditions'. The statement to the world's press read:

The exercise has been cancelled because of fog.

WEATHER OR NOT?

Even getting a general weather forecast can be a bit of a

problem for some authorities. In 1979, the *Arab News* in Saudi Arabia apologised to its readers that the country's meteorological centre had been unable to provide them with any information. The statement on the front page read:

We regret we are unable to give you the weather. We rely on weather reports from the airport, which is closed because of the weather. Whether we are able to give you the weather tomorrow depends on the weather.

SEEING THROUGH THE PROBLEM

The response of Teignmouth Council to a request for planning permission by local businessman, Derek Oram, made headlines in the English press in 1977. Mr Oram wanted to build a landing pad for a helicopter on the roof of his hotel, and had been sent a blank sheet of perspex and a note from the Planning Department. In reporting the application, the *Teignmouth Post and Gazette* said that an official of the department had told Oram:

Please reply on the enclosed form which has been printed by the Stronsky system of digital sine analysis. If you cannot understand the form, contact Mr Utter Nutter.

MANY HANDS MAKE LIGHT WORK

In 1978, an enquiry was instituted into the running of the Kenyan Civil Service. Government officials were particularly concerned about a report that over 85,000 names appeared on the Civil Service pay-roll. According to a report in *The Guardian*, when the head of the

Civil Service, Simon Nyachae, was asked to justify this figure, he explained:

The reason why 85,000 people appear on the list, who are, in actual fact, not on the Civil Service pay-roll, is the result of my attempt to discover if the states need extra hands.

CROSSED BY AUTHORITY

For several years the parents of children attending the Armour Valley School in the county of Connacht in Ireland lobbied the local authority to provide a traffic warden to supervise their children crossing the road to and from school. Each time the request came up for consideration it was turned down. The exasperated leader of the group of parents finally told the *Connacht Tribune* in October 1982:

The last time they turned us down was on the grounds that the warden's life would be in danger from passing cars.

SCHOOL LEAVE

The problem facing Gloucestershire Education Department in May 1985 was ostensibly one that many authorities have faced – the parents of a 12-year-old boy at Tonnerbridge School wanted him to be educated at home. The reason *why*, though, was far from ordinary and was explained by an official of the department, Arthur Waring, to *The Guardian*:

The boy suffers from scholastophobia, a very uncommon illness. For example, even the mention of the word 'school' makes him go berserk.

COFFEE HAS-BEANS

When US Congresswoman, Barbara Boxer, learned in 1984 that several hundred expensive coffee-makers had been purchased by the Pentagon, the Democrat from California put down a question in Congress. Why, she asked, had these items been bought at $7622 each when the same machines were on sale in Washington at just $99.50? *The Washington Post* quoted a Pentagon official's reply:

The brewer, which contains 2000 parts, makes ten cups of coffee and is to be installed in the Lockheed C5A. It is a very reliable device and will continue making coffee after loss of cabin pressure following a direct hit.

CAN'T SEE FOR DUST

In February 1984, Exeter City Council announced that it was replacing the 12 men who previously followed its dustcarts picking up litter with three mechanical sweepers. Despite complaints about the unemployment caused by this decision, a council official insisted to the *Devon and Somerset News* how efficient the new sweepers were. By noon on Monday, he said, they were over an hour ahead of the dustcarts and already picking up stray litter from the previous week's refuse. His excuse got even more grandiloquent:

In due time the sweepers will catch the dustcarts up – lapping them, you might say – and our studies show that passers-by may expect to see a dustcart being lapped by a sweeper at least once every three years.

HEART-STARTER

An ambulance driver and his colleague, who stopped for fish and chips while taking an emergency heart case to Standring Infirmary in November 1985, were in danger of losing their jobs, according to a report in *The Daily Telegraph*. Misdon Health Authority, for whom the two men worked, were requested to dismiss them for their behaviour – until their excuse was heard. A spokesman for the Authority said that the two men had been driving a Mr Eric Jenkins to the infirmary when they felt in need of food. After consulting with the patient, it was agreed that they would make a short detour to a fish bar owned by Mr Jenkins' grandmother in order to buy some chips. The Misdon statement added:

They chose Mr Jenkins' grandmother's shop because they would not have to queue. Having got the chips, they shared them with Mr Jenkins and on arrival there was no indication that the patient's condition had suffered.

DOWN THE TUBE

Bureaucracy at work in the world of television is legendary – but on one occasion at least, viewers might perhaps be grateful for the intervention of a TV mandarin. Or maybe not? The instance occurred when Grampian Television was in the process of being set up and its proposed title was to be Scottish Highlands and Islands Television. The man in question gently pointed out that station SHIT would hardly be appropriate! A spokesman for the Television Licensing Authority was also anxious to spare some blushes in April 1988 when he stated in a press release:

We have discouraged the incentive scheme, whereby prizes were given to those of our employees who brought the greatest number of prosecutions for non-possession of a licence, after two cases were brought against members of the public who are blind.

TOP-THAT TELEVISION

The failure of Live TV in October 1999 prompted some ill-concealed delight among the other television companies who had scoffed at the channel's attempt to win viewers with a character called 'News Bunny', Norwegian weather forecasts and a series called *Topless Darts*. When asked why it was being closed, chief executive, Kelvin MacKenzie, told *The Independent*:

We were three years ahead of our time.

THE BIG BANG

A long-standing mystery in American government circles about the whereabouts of some bomb-making materials was evidently no nearer a solution when an official was questioned in May 1988. The materials were part of a defence programme sponsored by the government at Oak Ridge, Tennessee, and it fell to the assistant manager of the programme, James Foutach, to provide an excuse *why* they had been missing for at least six years. The *Memphis Press-Scimitar* was just one of many papers to carry Foutach's reply:

They are missing, in that they cannot be found. We may find them under something else, or we may never find them. Maybe someone has made them into a bomb, or maybe they have not been made into a bomb. But you have to draw a line somewhere and we have reached the cost-benefit point where it simply does not pay us to keep looking.

AGE CONCERN

A derelict garage, which had been rented out by Cherwell District Council in Wiltshire, became an object of controversy in September 1986. After being used for several years by King Markets, there was strong local feeling that the building should be demolished. The council duly debated the matter but decided against the proposal. The *Devizes Herald* quoted a spokesman of the council:

The feeling was that it might be a suitable building to house old-age pensioners.

HOLD YOUR BREATH

In their turn, council officials are often the recipients of excuses from members of the general public. By far the majority of these are in connection with non-payment of council tax. It's rare, though, that they can take any-thing other than a very politically-correct line in res-ponding to excuses – although sometimes an element of humour may creep in, as it did in the case of Emborough Council, near Radstock in Somerset, which was reported by the *Bristol Evening Post* in February 1984. After a series of complaints from a Mr and Mrs George Snatsnell about the amount of condensation in their council flat, an official from the Housing Department was sent to investigate. In a subsequent letter to the Snatsnells, the man's suggestion was:

To restrain heavy night-time breathing on the part of your three children and yourselves.

A FOOT IN THE BACK PASSAGE

If you find *that* suggestion amusing, just consider the following selection of extracts from letters that have been received by officials of local councils all over Britain, and imagine how you might reply. And although the names of the writers have been omitted, every one is genuine.

- *Can you please tell me when our repairs are going to be done, as my wife is about to become an expectant mother.*
- *Will you please send a man to look at my water. It is a funny colour and not fit to drink.*
- *I wish to complain that my father hurt his ankle very badly when he put his foot in the hole in his back passage.*
- *I want some repairs doing to my cooker as it has backfired and burnt my knob off.*
- *Would you please send a man to repair my spit. I am an old age pensioner and need it straight away.*
- *I am writing on behalf of my sink which is running away from the wall.*
- *Our kitchen floor is very damp, we have two children and would like a third so will you please send someone to do something about it.*
- *I request your permission to remove my drawers in the kitchen.*
- *I am still having trouble with smoke in my built-in drawers.*
- *I awoke this morning and found my water boiling.*
- *The person next door has a large erection in his back garden, which is unsightly and dangerous.*

- *Will you please send me someone to mend our broken path. Yesterday my wife tripped and fell on it and she is now pregnant.*

Interestingly, the most frequent complaints of all to councils are about Thomas Crapper's pride and joy, the toilet. Here are my top six, each worthy of a 'Loo Papers' award:

- *The lavatory is blocked. This is caused by the house next door throwing their balls on the roof.*
- *The toilet is blocked and we cannot bath the children until it is cleared.*
- *Our lavatory seat is broken in half and is now in three pieces.*
- *This is to let you know that our lavatory seat is broken and we cannot get BBC2.*
- *Would you please repair our toilet, my son pulled the chain and the box fell on his head.*
- *The toilet seat is cracked – where do I stand?*

SICK OF ANSWERING

NHS Direct, the telephone help-line set up by the government which uses nurses to diagnose simple medical complaints and (hopefully) reduce the number of patients needing to visit surgeries, ran into trouble in December 1999 during a flu outbreak. So heavy was the number of calls to the phone centre serving Surrey, Sussex and parts of Kent, that the automated answering system broke down and was unable to provide information. According to a subsequent report in the specialist journal, *Doctor*, there was only one excuse that could be used to cope with the emergency:

The staff had to mimic the answering machines, reciting

an official message in breakdowns lasting hours at a time. If challenged by callers suspicious of stutters, stray coughs and background noise, the staff simply repeated the message like Daleks!

THE OUTLOOK IS BLANK . . .

The British Tourist Authority is, by its very nature, always on the look-out for ways of promoting the nation and its varied attractions. In July 2000, in the middle of yet another unseasonable period of wind and rain, a spokesman was asked by a BBC radio journalist why the Authority never referred to the weather in any of its brochures or reports. To which the official replied:

We don't feature the weather – it's not one of our selling points.

4

COP OUTS

It's the sight every motorist dreads – the wailing siren and flashing blue light in the mirror which means you've been speeding and the police want you to pull over. Getting nicked is a situation that is familiar to drivers and motorcyclists all over the world and exceeding the speed limit is just one of the rules of the road that get broken all the time. Some of these offences have inspired the most creative excuse-making as this chapter will reveal.

One of the very first accounts of going too fast on the nation's highways goes back to the early years of the twentieth century, when motoring was still in its infancy. The magazine *Motor and Motor Cycling* (which was launched in 1902 and which shortened its title to just *Motor* the following year) recorded a London motorist's excuse after a custodian of the law halted his drive along the Brighton Road: 'I was hurrying to find a garage before my car ran out of petrol.'

Back then it *might* have worked because petrol stations were few and far between. Today, though, it is necessary to be a bit more ingenious. One popular excuse I've been told can work is to look distressed, cross your legs and plead: 'I'm sorry, officer, I know I was speeding but I need to get to the loo badly.' It can apparently be doubly effective if you quickly ask for directions to the nearest convenience!

But for real ingenuity, take the case of the motorcyclist who was caught speeding near Poole in Dorset in October 1999. The rider was clocked at over 115 mph, according to a report in the *Dorset Evening Echo*, which added:

'He told the police he had just washed his bike and was trying to dry it.'

STAYED A LITTLE TOO LONG

In those days of yesteryear, even fines for parking could bring out the inventiveness in motorists. In 1933, a lady named Mrs Harriett Wood, who was apparently as beautiful as she was clever, escaped a fine in the small town of Tyler in Texas when she was brought before a venerable old judge for leaving her vehicle too long outside a dress shop. A report of the case in the *Houston Post* said she fluttered her eyelashes and smilingly confessed:

I'm afraid I was unavoidably detained in a girdle.

POOR COW

An early account of what amounted to road rage appeared in the *Detroit News* in 1938 when several motorists were arrested for breaking the law while trying to get out of a traffic jam. According to the newspaper, the chaos had been caused by a cow which had broken loose from one of the city's markets. The report continued with a dreadful howler:

Confused by the noise of traffic, a cow that probably was

experiencing its first taste of city life, got mixed up with vehicles in Milwaukee Avenue yesterday and was struck by a street car. It was so badly injured that Patrolman Stegmiller ended his life with a bullet.

THE RIGHT SIDE OF THE ROAD

Another equally amusing misprint appeared in the *Johannesburg Star* of South Africa in 1947. Reporting the evidence of an eye-witness to an accident caused by a motorcyclist going too fast in the city limits, the paper noted:

She could not say on which side of the road he was riding in Commissioner Street, but he turned into West Street on the wrong side. She was sure that after the accident she fell on to the pavement on the correct side of the road.

THE BEST EXCUSE BY A DISTANCE

In 1954, a columnist on *The Philadelphia Enquirer* claimed the best excuse he had ever heard given by a motorist pulled over for speeding went as follows:

I'm sorry, officer, I've been living in Europe for so many years that I have forgotten how to read the signs in miles per hour.

ABANDONED IN MID-STREAM

The driving test that Margaret Wilson took in Guildford, Surrey, in 1956 must be one of the most extraordinary on record, according to the *Daily Mail* report of events. It was Mrs Wilson's fifth test and things were going quite smoothly until she made a sharp left turn into Riverside Road. 'I'd just gone round the corner in first gear on full lock,' she explained later. 'I said to myself, "I'm too close to the edge," and then I must have put my foot on the accelerator instead of the brake because I went straight through the railings into the River Wey. The car started to sink. I had my window open and got on to the seat and half way out. The examiner opened his door and the water rushed in. Then he got out of the window.' The pair were, however, quickly rescued by a boat which happened to be sailing by and – the *Daily Mail* added – the examiner even managed to hang on to his briefcase and clipboard. A Ministry of Transport official said later:

As this was a terminated test, we cannot say whether the lady passed or failed until the examiner makes a report.

THE VOICE OF AUTHORITY

The *Daily Mail* also carried the story of another female learner driver who ran into trouble in September 1962. The woman stalled her car at a set of traffic lights and after a few moments other motorists behind began to hoot at her. However, directly behind was a police car and the officer inside switched on his loudspeaker and appealed to the other drivers to stop hooting as they were panicking the learner driver. Calmed by this, the woman waited until the lights changed again and then put her car into gear. According to the *Mail*, however, the hapless woman chose reverse and crashed straight into the police vehicle – from which a voice again issued over the loudspeaker:

Now look what the silly bitch has done.

LICENSED TO AMUSE

An Iowa farmer's wife who drove to a town near Des Moines in May 1963 to do some shopping was finding it difficult to park. Finally spotting a space between two vehicles, the lady endeavoured to manoeuvre her vehicle between them, first hitting one and then reversing into the other. According to a report of the subsequent court case in the *Des Moines Register*, the incident was witnessed by a police officer who asked her to step out from the badly dented car and produce her licence. With a bright smile she said:

Oh, don't be silly, officer. Who'd give me a licence?

THE PERFECT ANSWER

Among the many excuses that have been offered by drivers desperate to keep their licences when facing serious motorising offences, the most frequently heard is that the owner's livelihood depends on being able to drive. A judge sitting at the Liverpool Assizes in the 1960s is credited by the *Liverpool Weekly News* with having uttered this refute to one such plea:

And so do those of other motorists and pedestrians.

RAISING PAIN

The case of the courteous motorist who apparently raised his bowler hat after an accident came before the

St Albans Divisional Sessions in 1971. The man was summonsed for a driving offence, a report in the *Herts Advertiser & St Albans Times* stated, and during the proceedings he was asked by the prosecuting counsel, 'After the accident why did you raise your bowler hat to acknowledge the driver of the other car involved, when you did not know him?' To which the motorist replied:

The accident caused the hat to become crammed down over my eyes and ears, and although it might have been polite to raise it to the other driver, I lifted it to alleviate my discomfort.

IT'S THE WHEELS THAT COUNT

Overtaking in prohibited areas can land motorists in trouble. In 1978, a Loughborough citizen, Barnaby Stackhouse, was summonsed on just such a charge. According to an account of the court proceedings in the *Loughborough Echo*, Mr Stackhouse told the magistrates:

The no overtaking signs show a four-wheeled vehicle passing a four-wheeled vehicle. I was riding a motorcycle.

MY BUCKET'S GOT A GIRL IN IT

It wasn't the pillion passenger that John Dawes was seen carrying on his motorbike that got him into trouble with the police in Bournemouth, Dorset, in February 1980, but the fact that the girl was not wearing a crash helmet. Instead, she had a small iron bucket on her head. A report of the subsequent court case in the *Bournemouth Evening Echo* said that Mr Dawes explained to an officer:

The lady on the bike is my girlfriend, Veronica. A bucket suits her better than a helmet. We seek to combine fashion with caution.

MORE THAN MEETS THE EYE

Peter Kinnell, the author of the best-selling *Book of Erotic Failures* and its sequel, *More Erotic Failures*, tells the story of a policeman who was said to have made 'an unprofessional proposition' when he caught what he thought was an attractive policewoman breaking the speed limit in her car. But all was not as it seemed, Kinnell says:

When the woman unbuttoned her tunic to prove that she was actually a strippagram artiste in her popular 'WPC 69' outfit, the police constable withdrew his suggestion and booked her on the spot.

BACKWARD AT GOING FORWARD

After receiving a number of complaints about a car being driven around the streets of the town of Coeur d'Alene in Idaho in July 1980, a police patrol car arrived on the scene and stopped the vehicle. At the wheel was a teenage girl who told the officers that her parents had given her permission to drive the car, but she was afraid she had put too much mileage on the clock. According to an account of the incident in the *Oregonian*, the girl added:

I was just trying to unwind some of it.

THE STOP-START METHOD

Police checkpoints can throw up some pretty bizarre excuses from drivers. In July 1982, an Irish motorist whose car was stopped at a checkpoint in Derry was found to have no brakes on the vehicle whatsoever. The man, Keith Sherlock, was asked by the astonished officers how he had managed to drive the vehicle, let alone stop it. According to a report in the *Derry Journal*, he explained:

When I see a stop coming up I switch off the ignition, put the car into reverse, and then switch on the ignition again. It works, but you have to get the knack of it.

SPARK OF INTEREST

A motorist who was pulled over for speeding by a state trooper in Denver, Colorado, in 1982 was found to have several boxes of sparking plugs on the back seat of his car. When the man failed to give a satisfactory explanation as to where they had come from, he was arrested and subsequently his house was searched. There the police found over 290,000 more sparking plugs which, it transpired, he had stolen from the factory where he worked, according to a report in the *Denver Post*. Before being sentenced the man was asked if he could explain *why* he had stolen so many and replied:

I just like to see them around.

ON THE RUN

Among the list of speeding offences reported in the

Western Evening Herald of 12 May 1983, was a fine of £12 imposed by the Teignbridge Magistrates on Keith Robinson for driving a bus at 78 mph on the Chudleigh bypass. Admitting the offence, the defendant said:

The bus was carrying 20 prisoners from Dartmoor who were all anxious to reach the prison before it got dark.

MORE LIFTS THAN ONE!

The Yorkshire police officer had never seen a car quite like it before – the rear bumper of the vehicle was scraping along the road and the front wheels barely touched the surface. When the driver, David Hatchley, was brought to Hull Court in 1985 to face charges, his defending solicitor offered this excuse which was reported in the *Hull Daily Mail*:

My client was on the way home from an ice hockey conference when he saw a friend, George Thompson, walking along the lane and offered him a lift. As Mr Thompson was getting into the car, eleven other people, completely unknown to either of them, appeared out of nowhere, climbed into the back, and demanded to be driven to the nearest bus stop.

THE SHOCK OF SILENCE

Speed traps have produced their fair share of excuses over the years. A favourite among Gloucestershire police officers occurred in February 1986, when motorist, Christopher Gregory, was brought before Whitminster magistrates charged with driving at 98 mph through the trap. Asked to explain the reason – a report in the *Gloucestershire County Gazette* stated – Gregory answered:

I was driving my mother home from Manchester. I suddenly accelerated with surprise when, after two and a half hours of complete silence, she suddenly spoke to me.

QUICKER THAN THE EYE

A Scottish motorist brought before a Glasgow court in 1987, charged with speeding, was also said to have had no licence plate on the front of the vehicle. According to a report of the case in the *Glasgow Herald*, the driver told the officer who stopped him:

Aye, but I thought I was going fast enough so you wouldn't see.

DEAF TO APPEALS

The extraordinary case of a wife suing her husband for damages and negligence while travelling as a passenger in the couple's *own* car has been repeated at a number of solicitors' dinners, but may well be apocryphal. The hearing apparently took place in a London civil court, where it was stated that the husband was driving the car when he made a sudden right turn and his wife fell out of the other side. The man did not stop, however, but continued to the nearest emergency hospital where he demanded to see an ear specialist. When asked to explain his strange behaviour, the man standing in the dock replied:

I didn't know she'd fallen out – I thought I'd suddenly gone deaf.

POLICEMAN'S BALL HANGS IN THE BALANCE

Another story which probably has more than a little truth in it, although the details are not specific, is believed to have occurred in Kansas City, USA, in the 1970s. A woman who was stopped for speeding on a state highway thanked the trooper most profusely. When the officer asked *why* she was thanking him, the lady driver replied, 'It's the only way I could think of to get tickets for the Troopers' Ball.' At this the policeman replied:

Sorry, mam, but I can't get you any tickets because troopers don't have balls.

CARRIED AWAY BY THE MUSIC

After being stopped for speeding at over 100 mph on the outskirts of London in January 1988, a former army officer, Major Christopher Gilding, gave this excuse to police officers, according to a report of the subsequent court proceedings carried by *The Times*:

I had Beethoven on the player – Wellington's Victory March. Suddenly there came the great bugle call, the cavalry under Lord Uxbridge brought up Ponsonby's Cavalry Brigade and away we went! Slap down between Papelotte and Le Hale Sainte and bang into d'Eleron's Infantry . . . I plead guilty. I gave my horse its head. In the heat of the moment I failed to notice the police car behind me.

THESE SHOES ARE MADE FOR EXCUSES

Wearing the latest fashion in shoes was 17-year-old Rosemary Smith's excuse when she was brought before the magistrates at Harlow in Essex in March 1999, charged with speeding. According to a report of the case in the *West Essex Gazette*, the girl told the officers who stopped her for doing over 85 mph:

These platform shoes I'm wearing are very heavy. They weigh my feet down and I was going fast because they were pulling my foot down.

A KNOTTY CASE

Northumberland Magistrates Court was told in October 1999 that a female driver had been stopped after driving at speeds in excess of 105 mph near Newton-on-the-Moor. Her excuse was given in an account of the case published by the *Birmingham Evening Mail*:

I got carried away listening to a programme on the radio about knitting.

THE NET RESULT

Recently, a number of excuses which, it is claimed, have been successfully employed to escape fines for motoring offences have been posted on the internet. The three most original – and amusing – I have seen are all on an American site, 'Submit Excuses', to which I make due acknowledgement:

• *Sorry, officer, I was leading in the Indianapolis 500 . . .*

but I think I took a wrong turn!

- *Please excuse me from this speeding ticket. My wife ran off with a state policeman and when I saw your flashing lights I didn't stop because I thought you might be the trooper trying to bring her back to me!*
- *I have a very pretty blonde friend whose name is Athena. She was stopped late one evening by a Texas state trooper who actually used the line, 'OK, lady, where's the fire?' The reply that got her off a ticket? 'Oh, officer, in your eyes!'*

A POLICE SPOKESMAN SAID – 1

The police themselves have, of course, been known to resort to using their own excuses on occasions – the Irish especially. In April 1978, the *Sunday Independent* ran a story from Ireland about a prisoner, Robert Wilson, who had escaped from police custody in Dublin while he was in the process of being charged with killing a man. Asked for a comment on the escape, a spokesman in the Gardai press office told the newspaper:

Wilson is no more dangerous than any other murderer.

A POLICE SPOKESMAN SAID – 2

Another Gardai spokesman also found himself in the hot seat in September 1981, when he was being questioned about a bank raid in Limerick. According to a report in the *Irish Independent*, the man was asked to explain why the murder squad detectives had failed to identify the body of one of the armed robbers who had been accidentally shot by one of the other members of the gang during the raid. He responded:

The fact that a number of detectives saw the corpse but could not put a name to it is understandable if you bear in mind that it was still masked.

A POLICE SPOKESMAN SAID – 3

The third policeman to provide the members of the press with a classic moment of humour was a spokesman in Belfast. The man was giving details in February 1984 to journalists, including a representative of *The Guardian*, about the intensive search that was going on for a van containing surveillance equipment and secret documents which had been stolen. He added:

Our search is being hampered by the fact that the van is a Special Branch vehicle and they do not wish to issue a description of it to the public.

GETTING A HANDLE ON CRIME

A police spokesman for Guernsey Police was very happy to announce in March 1981 that the government of the second largest of the Channel Islands had authorised them to spend £4,000 on special X-ray equipment. The man was quoted in the *Guernsey Weekly Press* as saying:

Police officers will no longer have to stand behind a garden wall and open suspicious objects with a pair of long-handled garden shears.

MAKE WAY FOR THE DUKE

Here, to round off this section, is the story of a writer for *Country Life* magazine who found himself receiving a breathless excuse from a policeman when he visited Buckingham Palace to interview the Duke of Edinburgh in May 2000. Just as the man was entering the gates of the palace, the policeman frantically waved him to one side as the Duke roared through at the wheel of his Land Rover. According to an account of the incident in *The Times*, the officer of the law told the writer:

Sorry about that, sir. The Duke never usually stops.

5

HARD TO SWALLOW!

There's an old joke much loved by comedians: 'I don't drink and drive – the bumps make me spill too much.' Drink-driving is, of course, quite rightly frowned on today. But there are still those drivers one pint short of a gallon who take to the roads with a skinful and then try to talk their way out of trouble when they are caught and breathalysed. Some of the excuses offered in these circumstances will be found in the following pages – and let's begin with what has been aptly called the lamest excuse of all for drunken driving.

The story concerns a graphic artist, Garry Livingstone, who collided with another vehicle while driving home from a wedding reception in August 1984. According to a report in *The Daily Telegraph*, he was breathalysed and charged with having excess alcohol in his blood. At Bristol Crown Court his solicitor asked for the conviction to be set aside because his client had only one leg.

'Although he drove with twice the legal amount of alcohol, he has less blood than a person with two legs and was therefore more greatly under the influence.'

SHOME MISHTAKE, SHURELY? – 1

In February 1976, a charge of drunken driving heard in a court in Iowa generated a lengthy debate on the extent of the motorist's intoxication – as well as a very surprising outcome. A report in *The New York Times* described the evidence which was provided about the man by the police who had arrested him and two doctors who had examined him later in hospital. In ordering that the case should be dismissed, the judge said:

The defendant was clearly too drunk to have consented to the blood alcohol test that proved he was inebriated.

SHOME MISHSTAKE, SHURELY? – 2

An equally bizarre story has been reported in Britain. It is claimed to be based on an actual incident though I have been unable to find any references to it in newspaper reports or court proceedings. It concerns a man who staggered from a public house and began fumbling with the keys to his car. A policeman standing nearby watched the driver's hopeless attempts to get into the vehicle for several minutes. Finally, the officer walked over to the car and said to the man that he hoped he was not going to drive. At this, back came the excuse:

Shertainly I am, offisher. I'm too bloody drunk to walk.

THE IRISH IMAGINATION

When Finbar Malone was arrested on suspicion of being a drunken driver in July 1978, his subsequent appearance at Hammersmith Magistrates Court provided copy for several newspapers, including the *Irish Post* which ran the saga in full. According to the prosecutor, Mr George Wembridge, when Malone was stopped by the police he told the officers that his wife had just died at home. A nurse had given him something to drink in order to settle his nerves while he drove to fetch his brother-in-law, a Catholic priest, to administer the last rites. But, said Mr Wembridge, the story was rather different when the defendant was taken to the police station.

There he told the duty officer that he had been thrown into the street by three bailiffs and had had to take a drink in order to steady his nerves while he went to fetch his cousin who was a lawyer. However, when the time came for Mr Malone to make a statement, he said that he had been told to go at top speed to Hammersmith to fetch some morphine for his son who had broken his leg after falling off a rocking horse. On investigation, it was found that Mrs and Master Malone were both alive and well and they had not been evicted.

BLURRED VISION

A car which two amazed policemen stopped in Bournemouth, Dorset, in October 1978 had a thick coat of green paint on both the windscreen and back window. According to an account of the subsequent events in the *Western Mail*, the driver, Mr Stephen Holton, admitted to the officers that he had been drinking, but because the day was 'a bit misty' he had decided to attempt to drive home. The car, however, was not his own. In recounting his version of events in court, Mr Holton called a neighbour, Mr James Cunningham, who admitted that he had painted the windows of the car. Mr Cunningham then explained:

I painted the windows of my girlfriend's father's car. He had been telling his daughter bad things about me. It just so happens that her father and Mr Holton drink in the same pub and both men have the same sort of car . . .

THE WILDER WEST

A driver stopped by police going the wrong way down a well-signposted one-way street in Detroit, Michigan, in 1980 was clearly drunk according to the police officer who arrested him. When the officer subsequently appeared in court, the *Detroit News* quoted the policeman's statement:

I soon realised he was intoxicated. I asked him if he had seen the arrows and he replied, 'I didn't even see the Indians.'

BARKING MAD?

In July 1986, the *Intelligencer Journal* of Pennsylvania reported that a blind man, W D Bowen of Louisville in Kentucky, had been charged with drunken driving. According to the newspaper, Mr Bowen had attended the local court to deny the offence on the grounds of his blindness and that his dog, named Bud, had actually been in charge of the vehicle! He explained to the judge that the animal – who sat in the passenger seat beside him – had been trained to bark once for a red light and twice when it turned green. If other cars around him were going faster, Mr Bowen explained, Bud would rap his tail on his owner's leg – once if he was going too slowly and twice if too fast. Presenting the evidence against Mr Bowen, police officer Doug Willwood told the court that he had seen the car change lanes every 10 seconds during the time he had been following it. The officer added:

That's why I charged Mr Bowen. And Bud is not tall enough to see the white lines on the highway.

ONE EXCUSE DESERVES ANOTHER . . .

Not one excuse would do for a London driver when he was arrested for drunken driving in January 1988; he offered a whole series of them. In a report in the *Star* newspaper, Gifford Russell said that he took deep exception to being labelled by the officer who arrested him as 'the most sodden person I have ever seen at the wheel'. Protesting his innocence, Russell told the magistrates at Marylebone Court:

After a telephone call from the landlord of the Four Pelicans saying that my wife needed a lift, we were stopped just after I had picked her up. My speech was slurred because I have a speech impediment. My eyes were glazed because I was wearing my new contact lenses. I could not walk a straight line because after many years at sea I have a naturally rolling gait. My steering was not quite true because my wife was trying to seize the wheel. And I smelled of drink because she threw a pint of cider over me as I was leading her out of the Pelicans.

There is no point in trying to top that, I think!

6

COURT OUT

It is not only motoring offences and drink-driving that our courts have to deal with, and the press bears witness to the fact that excuses have been paraded just as thick and fast for a variety of other misdemeanours. Here again, when answering charges, defendants and their solicitors have displayed an inventiveness that has sometimes been nothing short of hilarious. Take, for example, the case in 1977 of a man who appeared before London magistrates charged with stealing a household gas meter. He had been arrested by the police after being seen leaving a pub with the cumbersome object in his arms. When asked by the chairman of the bench to explain, he replied:

Well, your honour, I was asked by this smart boy in the bar if I would like to buy the newest type of transistor radio complete with all the latest dials for £5. I thought it seemed a good buy!

Here are some more examples of this same kind of excuse-me in court.

A WEIGHTY RESPONSE

Another man caught with an unlikely object in his arms came up before magistrates in Sutton, Surrey, in

September 1948. William Carr was charged with being found early one morning carrying away a heavy iron gate hinge from the premises of Messrs James, Croydon and Thompson. When asked by the arresting officer why he had the hinge – a report in the *Sutton Times* stated – Carr replied:

I was going to make a bird cage.

THE REASON OF LAW

A fine display of Irish wit was recorded by the *Kerryman* in August 1949, when a farmer appeared before a local court to answer a series of charges. The man had opted to conduct his own defence and when asked by the magistrate whether he was guilty or not, replied:

Indeed, I'm innocent, your honour. To be sure, if I was guilty I would have found myself a lawyer.

NO SMOKE WITHOUT FIRE

Brazilian André Le Riche became notorious in the 1950s for committing acts of indecency in Rio de Janeiro. He was several times brought to court for exposing himself and making lewd gestures at women. In June 1956, after several warnings that any further appearances in court would result in a long prison sentence, Le Riche was once again before the justices. This time he had been caught by the police on the roof of a house, according to a report in *Edio Republican*, and when asked what he was doing claimed:

I thought the house was alight so I was pissing down the chimney to extinguish the fire.

NO CORRUPTION WITHOUT COPS

A few years later, another Brazilian, Joao Damico, described as 'Brazil's most successful car thief' was surprisingly cleared of a series of theft charges in San Paolo. Giving an interview to the *Brazil Herald* about what he saw as the 'threat' to his title, Damico said:

I do not understand the world any more. Perhaps I am suffering from hallucinations. I have been a car thief for 25 years and this is the first time police officers have refused a bribe of several million cruzeiros to let me get off. I am seriously disappointed by this unpatriotic behaviour.

DRESSED TO IMPRESS

A man arrested after holding up an expensive tailor's shop in Kansas City, USA, in September 1957 was anything but a picture of sartorial elegance. Martin Williams was wearing an old sports shirt, dirty khaki trousers and scuffed brown shoes. When brought before a local court he asked for three other counts of holding up tailors' shops in order to steal suits to be taken into account. His excuse was reported in the *Kansas City Kansan*:

I wanted to look presentable enough to rob a bank. If I went in looking like I usually do, they would suspect me right away.

NO CHANGE THERE

In June 1959, office worker Jan Raha of Prague was arrested by police on charges of fraud. When his trial came to court, a report in the *Mlada Fronta* stated that the officers had asked Raha how approximately £27,000 of his employer's money had disappeared. He exclaimed that the whole thing was a mistake and added:

I must have accidentally mixed it up with some of my own loose change.

PULL THE OTHER ONE

It seemed like a fair cop when police in Niles, California, arrested a man in the act of committing a burglary in October 1962. According to a report in the *Oakland Tribune*, he was asked to explain why he was in possession of a crowbar, file, hacksaw and screwdriver. His reply was later read out in court:

They are vital maintenance tools to keep my artificial leg in working order.

SOMETHING THEY ATE?

The brothel run by the two sisters, Delfina and Maria Gonzalez, in Mexico City, was well known to satisfied clients – and the police. But following yet another raid in 1964, the body of one of their girls was found half-buried in the garden. Further investigation uncovered the remains of another 80 prostitutes, ran a story in *La Aficion*. The Gonzalez sisters were arrested by police and taken to court where Delfina was asked for an explanation about all the bodies:

Maybe the food didn't agree with them.

A FINE COCK-UP!

The Reverend Jessie Jessup appeared in court in Gulfport, Mississippi, in November 1964 to face a variety of charges that had been brought against him. It was alleged that he had used the offerings to his church to buy cars, boats, sea planes and even fighting cocks. According to a report in the *New York Daily News*, the court was told that the Reverend had been married four times, obtained two divorces by making false statements, and married a fourth wife – who was only 15 – while he was still married to the third. After the evidence had been presented, his assistant clergyman stated:

We feel there must be some kind of misunderstanding.

PRESSED FOR MONEY

Another man of the church who found himself in trouble with the law was Father Guido Antonelli, who ran a small parish on the outskirts of Rome. In February 1979, the police raided the church and found the Father in a cellar below the building working at a small printing press, said a report in *Giornale D'Italia*. Stacked around the room were piles of forged 50,000 lire notes. The Father excused himself to the police:

I had to make them because the church collections were so poor.

BARKING UP THE RIGHT TREE

In 1968, a Police Constable Dolan was commended by Kensington Magistrates Court for the part he had played in arresting a dangerous criminal. The officer had managed to persuade the cornered villain to give himself up by imitating the bark of a police dog. The *London Evening Standard* carried the story with a postscript by PC Dolan:

We used to have a dog, but had to get rid of it as an economy measure.

BOXED IN ON ALL SIDES

Cheshire Police Sergeant Stanley Minshall was startled to see a woman lying screaming inside a telephone kiosk as he passed by in November 1969. A man, whom the Sergeant later learned was her husband, was also in the box and Minshall opened the door and asked him what was the matter. At this the husband began to attack the officer and his wife also joined in. When the case came to court, the *Birkenhead News* printed Inspector R Jones's comment to the magistrate:

This is a classic example of what sometimes happens when a police officer tries to stop a husband striking his wife.

ADDING A TOUCH OF GLOSS

After being arrested in the spring of 1970 for being in possession of almost 5,000 lipsticks, George Mantova of Tasmania, Australia, appeared before a local court. He was jailed for six months – despite the excuse he gave to the judge which was reported in the *Hobart Mercury*:

They were all for my girlfriend.

PROVIDING FOR ONE AND ALL

Another busy thief appeared before magistrates in Chicago in 1973 charged with stealing huge numbers of items of clothing. The *Chicago Tribune* listed these in descending order as 800 pairs of socks, 757 sweaters, 733 shirts, 460 women's dresses, 403 men's jackets and 286 pairs of trousers. When asked the reason for amassing this haul, Gideon Howe replied:

I have a large family.

THE RUBBER BARON

When police were called to a copse of trees near Ealing, London, in the autumn of 1974, they found a man dressed from head to foot in rubber hiding behind some bushes. According to a report in the *News of the World*, the man, Matthew Grey, was wearing a red rubber dress, a black rubber brassière, two rubber belts, black rubber gloves and a rubber cloak. He also had on a blonde wig. Later, when brought to court, Grey, a bachelor in his fifties, said:

I had had a very bad day.

AN UNCONTROLLABLE URGE

The pretty girls of Hong Kong provided an attraction that Li Cheung found difficult to resist – so much so that in April 1976, he found himself before a local court on a charge of indecent assault. After the facts of the case had been outlined by the police and Cheung had given his version of events, the magistrate, Michael Hill, sentenced him to nine months' imprisonment and – according to the *South China Morning Post* – concluded:

I do not accept the excuse that your thumb has had an irresistible pinching impulse since childhood.

ALL JUICED UP

Although 81-year-old Elvira Thomas was considered a strong and lively woman for her age, the other residents in a nursing home where she lived in Willits, California, were still staggered when she was accused of beating to death her 85-year-old husband in 1977. An account of the killing and the subsequent trial was carried by the *Los Angeles Times*, complete with a quote from a member of the staff of the home who said:

She drinks a lot of carrot juice.

THE KNOCKOUT JUDGE

Judge Nathan Heffer was known as a scourge of serial criminals in his court at Passaic, New Jersey. In 1977, James Driver was brought before him and admitted to having carried out over 200 muggings. At this, said a report in the *New York Post*, the judge stood up from the bench, crossed the floor to where Driver was standing awaiting sentence, and punched him on the nose. As he strode back to the bench Judge Heffer snapped out:

That is an example of honest police brutality. I suggest you apply for a retrial on those grounds.

A TRIP ON HIGH

Police in Patrai in Greece were astonished to discover that a 73-year-old nun, Sister Panope Flothee, had been smoking pot. Taken before a local court in August 1980, she was charged with planting, nurturing and, at a later date, smoking cannabis in the garden of her convent. A report of the proceedings published in the *Athens News* quoted the nun as saying:

The plants enable me to participate with greater fervour in my prayers. I did not plant the seeds: God's breeze wafted them into the garden.

HEAD CASE

It was one of the most grisly scenes local police officers had ever come across, according to an account in the *Poona Herald* in April 1980. An elderly woman was found lying in a pool of blood with her head completely severed from her body. The following day when Vela Velayudhan was brought before a local court charged with beheading his mother-in-law he explained:

We had not been getting along for some time.

SERVICE WITH A VENGEANCE

The bar of the Scotia Lounge in Aberdeen was busy as usual in January 1981. But the action of one customer landed him in court, a report in the *Aberdeen Evening Express* stated. The man, Murray Clyde, was charged with possessing an offensive weapon – a hatchet – which he had swung above his head before bringing it crashing down on to the edge of the bar. Asked the reason, he told the police:

I was having difficulty in catching the barmaid's eye.

HIS FLEXIBLE FRIEND

The extraordinary story of Elmer Copehaver, an inmate of Bowden Prison in Alberta, Canada, who had obtained 83 credit cards while serving five years for fraud, emerged during a court case in May 1982. Reported by the *Calgary Herald*, the facts were given by Harry Stanley, defending counsel for the prisoner, who denied the charge that his client had obtained the credit cards by using 57 false names and was intent on a criminal purpose. The lawyer insisted:

Mr Copehaver has assured me that he is working on a thesis about the use and abuse of credit cards and is hoping to earn a master's degree in business administration.

THE CRIMINAL CODE

During a major prosecution case of several gangland figures at the Old Bailey in London in July 1982, a police officer told the presiding judge that five witnesses would not be appearing to give evidence. According to an account in the *London Evening Standard*, the officer explained that one of these had been shot dead, another had been dismembered, and a third had died from an overdose of drugs. A fourth man had died of drink and the fifth had vanished from a girlfriend's house just minutes before two policemen had arrived to bring him to the court. The officer added:

However, we are satisfied there are no suspicious circumstances.

JUMPING FOR FREEDOM

After being on the run from a California prison for several days, convicted burglar Glenn Kalina was recaptured by Los Angeles law officers and taken before a judge. But before being sentenced to a further three years – a report in the *Los Angeles Times* in March 1983 stated – Kalina was asked how he had managed to escape:

I was practising pole vaulting in the prison yard when I fell over the wall. I tried to find the gate to get back in again, but being unfamiliar with the area, I found myself in a town thirty miles away.

(NB. The world record for the pole vault is 6.14 metres (over 20 feet): the prison walls in question were 25 feet tall.)

SURVIVAL KIT?

When James Course of Winthorpe, near Newark-on-Trent, was searched by police officers in April 1984, he was found to be carrying a knuckleduster and thus charged with being in possession of an offensive weapon. The *Daily Mail* reported the case and also quoted the excuse he gave to the judge:

I have been studying knuckleduster technique in order to help my family survive after a nuclear war.

A QUESTION OF IDENTITY

When Edward Haddington was arrested after stealing six pounds of potatoes from a supermarket in Dundee, the police were surprised to find that he had his name tattooed across his forehead. The curious reason for this was explained in court and reported in June 1986 by the *Dundee Courier*:

I did not think anyone would be able to identify me because I do my own tattooing. But as I used a mirror for my forehead I got the lettering back to front.

MIRROR IMAGE

Another instance of identity crisis occurred a few years earlier, in November 1981, when J W Watson of Pinchbeck in Lincolnshire was arrested for breaking a shop window with his head. When the case came to court, PC Brian Brine gave the defendant's reason for the incident, as reported in the *Spalding Guardian*:

As I passed the window I saw my reflection and formed the impression that I was about to be attacked by a vicious assailant, whereupon I charged.

STRIPPED TO THE BONE

There was a considerable interest among the tabloid press journalists when Yvonne Bullen, a porno movie star, appeared at Bow Street Magistrates Court in 1983. The actress was charged with shoplifting and her excuse to the bench was reported by *The Sun*:

I just didn't know what I was doing. It has been nothing

but work, work, work for the last two years. In over 30 sex films I have performed over 2000 erotico-gymnastic acts. You can see I am dazed by it all because the goods for which I forgot to pay were all dog foods for my Alsatian, 'Casanova', who I poisoned by mistake last week.

LOVE IN THE GALLERY

The judge in the Aberdeen court found the distraction caused by a man and woman in the public gallery rather more than he was prepared to permit, according to a report in *The Scotsman* in November 1985. The couple were apparently making love and so the judge halted proceedings. The newspaper account continued:

Summoned before the bench, Miss Mary Favour explained that she could not give the judge the name of her boyfriend. 'I only met him an hour ago,' she said.

BANGERS AND CRASH

When a second-hand car dealer appeared before Swansea magistrates in September 1987 for selling a car described as 'a good roadworthy vehicle', the truth proved to be very different. Reporting the case, the *South Wales Echo* said the police had established the car was actually made up from four vehicles which had been 'rather badly welded together and given a quick spray job'. Asked if he had anything to say before sentence was passed, the defendant replied:

Well, no second-hand car is perfect.

DIGGING UP THE TRUTH

The courthouse in Kinsey, Alabama, was packed in December 1993 when a local woman was charged with tampering with a tomb in the local graveyard. Rumours of black magic and voodoo preceded the appearance of Diana Smith, according to the *Birmingham Post-Herald*, but the facts were much more bizarre. The judge heard that the woman had been found digging up the body of a man whose death she had been charged with causing in 1990. Pleading guilty to the new charge of tampering with the grave, she said:

I was just digging up the casket to prove that he was faking it.

HENPECKED TO DEATH

A 76-year-old South African, Nimrod Nbini, was charged in Cape Town in July 1994 with killing a penguin on one of the town's beaches. According to a report in the *Cape Times*, Nbini claimed in court that he had never seen a penguin before, and added:

It pecked my leg and I thought it would kill me. I believed it was a killer chicken.

TENDER MERCIES?

During the summer of 1994, the Great Lakes area of North America was the focal point of a number of brutal killings until, in the September, three men were arrested. The men were brought to court in November and all were given life sentences. Reporting the proceedings, the *Milwaukee Journal* said that one of the accused, Frederick Treesh, tried to excuse the trio while he was in the witness box:

Other than the two we killed, the two we wounded, the woman we pistol-whipped, and the light bulbs we stuck in people's mouths, we didn't really hurt anybody.

SORELY TRIED

In 1996, Anthony St Laurent of Providence, Rhode Island, admitted to taking part in organised crime. After a brief trial, he was found guilty and sentenced to ten months' imprisonment. As soon as the sentence had been handed down, however, St Laurent claimed that he was completely innocent of the charge. The *Providence Journal* quoted his revelation to the court:

The only reason I entered a guilty plea was because I'm suffering from an illness that means I have to take 40 to 50 enemas a day. It would have been real difficult to sit through a long trial.

NO SWEET ENDING

As part of a campaign against litter, a number of people were brought before the magistrates at Knottingly, Humberside, in October 1996. Among them was Colin Cleveland who was fined £25 for dropping an empty tube of Smarties into the River Wyre. A report in the *Hull Evening Mail* said that Cleveland's girlfriend, Wendy Jenkins, had tried to excuse his actions in her statement:

He had been trying to throw Smarties into my mouth all

afternoon. But when he had so little success he threw the packet into the river in a gesture of despair.

THE FAT OF THE LAND

According to a report in *The Washington Post* in November 1996, the US Supreme Court had rejected the appeal of a convicted Arizona drug-dealer who had demanded a retrial on the most unusual grounds. His reason?

I did not receive a fair trial because there were no fat people on the jury.

DRESSED TO KILL

In January 2000, a Philadelphia man was charged with attempting to rob a local bank at gunpoint. According to the *Philadelphia Evening Bulletin*, the man had entered the bank dressed as an elderly woman, pulled a pistol from a handbag and demanded money from a cashier. He was arrested while fleeing from the scene and later tried to excuse his appearance and actions in these curious words:

I did it because I am suffering from cultural insanity brought about by long-term exposure to racism.

7

TAXED TO THE HILT

The claim by Laslo Benko for a rebate of £2000 on his income tax must rate as one of the most unusual excuses ever offered to the revenue authorities. It happened in Gothenburg, Sweden, in 1983, when Benko claimed on his tax return that the money had been used in an effort to alleviate his 'abnormally severe depressions'. It had all been spent on prostitutes, he said.

The case, which was headlined in the *Goteborg Aftonposten* as 'Happiness is a Girl and a Tax Cut', was reported in August 1984. According to the paper, Benko had told the tax authorities, 'I need girls to keep my depression under some form of control,' and had supported his claim by quoting sub-sections in the tax regulations which allowed rebates to those suffering from long-term illness. But, doubtful as to whether the man's depressions could be defined as a long-term illness, the local tax inspector had turned the matter over to his superiors, who were equally baffled and decided to take the case to court for a ruling.

The *Goteborg Aftonposten* continued: 'In court Laslo argued that he should have equal rights with other groups and quoted cases where people had been allowed rebates because the treatment of their illness involved buying more expensive food, special clothing or having to travel. He produced letters from his doctor confirming the serious depressions and stated that recently there had been a 'distinct improvement' in his condition. But there was no medical evidence to say whether or not the improvement was due to Laslo's girlfriends and the court ruled that he had 'no significant cause' to be allowed a tax rebate.

When Benko decided to take the case to the Court of Appeals, he had no further luck, but the comment of the judge, Kjell Nystrand, is a classic of jurisprudence . . . and comedy:

The difficulty is to prove that the illness makes a substantial incursion into 'normal' living and to decide what expenses are permissible as 'additional' and beyond that 'norm'. The normal procedure is for a patient to provide specified receipts for inspection by the tax officers. I imagine it would be rather difficult to produce receipts from prostitutes and, if such were available, it would raise other rather ridiculous aspects such as VAT, employers' taxes and income taxes to be levied on the prostitutes.

BLAST THE EFFICIENCY

In that same year of 1984, the United States Revenue Service issued a document concerning nuclear warfare. The department had conducted a survey into the effects a nuclear strike might have on America and the normal process of gathering taxes. The paper concluded with the statement:

Many taxpayers will be inconvenienced by the hostilities and will have to be excused from paying the normal rates of interest on their debts.

MANY A SLIP . . .

Back in the years immediately following the Second World War, when attitudes were rather different from those today, the IRS in Washington received a typed income tax return from a bachelor in Michigan who listed one dependent son. According to a report in the *Gould Battery News*, a tax examiner returned the form with a pencil note: 'This must be a stenographic error.' The form was very promptly returned with another notation beneath:

You're telling me!

PRAYING FOR RELIEF

An Irish farm labourer, John Murphy of Tipperary, was relentlessly pursued by the local authorities to pay his taxes during the early 1950s. After a string of verbal excuses to officers who visited his cottage, the man finally agreed to complete his tax form in 1956. After filling in his name and address, the man added with no further word of explanation:

Filling in a tax form is against my religion.

AN ESTIMABLE METHOD

The British comedy writer Sid Green, who wrote for many TV stars including Eric Morecambe and Ernie Wise, and was later a scriptwriter in America for the *Johnny Carson Show*, told the story of a friend in the entertainment business who returned a tax form to the Inland Revenue which had asked for an estimate of his income – but deliberately left off his name and address. Recounting the facts to a reporter from the *Radio Times* in 1969, Green said his friend's excuse was:

If they want me to guess how much I'm going to make next year, they can guess who sent it!

THUMBS DOWN

In 1979, the Minister of Pensions in Malaya, Datuk Ibrahim, reported a remarkable fraud in which the thumbs of dead people were being used to secure pay-outs from the government. Speaking from his office in Kuala Lumpur to the *Singapore Sunday Times*, Ibrahim explained how the scam worked:

The embalmed thumb fraud has been costing the government over a million dollars a year. The rogues amputate the thumbs of dead pensioners, mark their pension-books with the thumbprint, and continue to draw their pensions. When we discovered this dreadful crime, 567 pensioners died of a mysterious epidemic in three days.

THE LAST POST

When George Blanksten, a professor of political science at Northwestern University in Chicago, filled in his tax return in 1984 and as part of this asked for a rebate on a medical bill, he was not prepared for the response he got from the US Social Security Administration. For they refused the claim on the grounds that he was dead! Recounting the story, the *Chicago Tribune* said that the administration had Blanksten's death logged in their computers as 6 August 1984. The poor man was therefore forced to go through an entire appeals procedure in order to try and reverse the official decision of his demise. Some months later, the SSA told the professor it had reviewed 'whether our original determination was correct' and had decided it was and he wasn't. Almost in despair, Blanksten recruited his Congressman and the columnist Mike Ryko to confirm he *was* still in the land of the living and actually teaching 200 students every day. Finally, said the *Chicago Times*, on Tuesday 17 September 1985 he received a letter from the SSA:

We are pleased to confirm that, as of today's date, your existence has been re-entered by our computers. We are sorry for any inconvenience this has caused you.

DEAD RECKONING

Seven years later, a British taxpayer, David Foskett, made use of this idea in reverse – although what he did was later described by the magistrates at Stroud Court in Gloucestershire as a 'serious and deliberate fraud'. An account of the proceedings in the *Stroud News & Journal* of January 1992 said that although Foskett had obtained £700 in income support from the DSS, he had at the same time tried to avoid paying his poll tax of just over £200 by claiming he was dead. How he tried to make this ploy work was read out to the court by the prosecuting counsel:

During a nostalgic trip to Horton Road Hospital, Mr Foskett came across an old Death Certificate which he filled in with his own name and sent off to the District Council.

REASONABLE CAUSES?

Professor John Ryesky who served for many years as an attorney for the IRS in America has amassed quite a collection of excuses offered by taxpayers. He says that avoiding tax has been a popular pursuit for years and that the provisions of Section 6651 of the United States Internal Revenue Code *almost* provides an excuse for doing so. It specifies penalties for failing to pay up unless a person can show that the reason is 'due to reasonable cause and not due to wilful neglect'. Here are some of Professor Ryesky's favourites:

- *Payment of income tax is voluntary.*
- *I refuse to file the tax return on the grounds that it violates my Fifth Amendment rights.*
- *The Tax Law is unenforceable because the symbol '$' used to specify taxes is undefined and ambiguous.*
- *I had a back pain.*
- *The Paperwork Reduction Act relieves Americans of their duty to file tax returns.*
- *I didn't file my tax return because I am an illegal alien.*

MAKING A MEAL OF IT

Civil servant George Barnes, who worked for the Inland Revenue in Britain until the late 1980s, has also collected a number of comical excuses from taxpayers on this side of the Atlantic. Among the most amusing examples he came across are:

- *My dog ate all my tax documents.*
- *I earn so little I cannot even afford to eat.*
- *I have decided to become a tramp.*
- *The Inland Revenue just does not understand my situation.*

- *I cannot pay because my wife has just run off with my bank manager.*
- *I am feeling very depressed.*

BARRED FROM PAYING

In 1999, according to a report in *The American Lawyer*, a group of prisoners in a US jail filled in tax returns in which they claimed a number of refunds. When these were surprisingly authorised, the men had their wives and girlfriends cash the cheques. However, the deception was discovered and all four were ordered to repay the sums of money. One of the group, David Hicks, tried unsuccessfully to appeal against the sentence, the report adds, and wrote to the authorities:

I will not be able to find employment to pay the restitutions after I am released from custody because I am indigent, inexperienced and I have a criminal record.

8

OFF THE STRAIGHT AND NARROW

There's nothing very funny about a car accident – until it comes to filling in an insurance claim. The files of major insurance companies all over the world contain the most amazing excuses from drivers trying to explain the mangled pieces of machinery that were once their pride and joy.

Among some of the most regular claims are those for vehicles found damaged after being left in a multi-storey car park, a supermarket car park or at a railway station. One favourite excuse which has been noted in different variations as far afield as Britain, Europe, America, Australia and New Zealand goes something like this. A car owner returns to his vehicle which he had left in a shopping centre car park to find it badly dented and scratched. Stuck under the windscreen wiper is a note that momentarily raises his spirits until he reads what is written:

The people who saw this happen are now watching me and think that I am writing down my name and address and that of my insurance company on this piece of paper. I'm not.

A STANDING JOKE!

Another classic excuse which has reportedly been given to several international insurers – particularly vehicle rental companies – is a variation of these words:

I collided with a stationary vehicle coming the other way.

FOR FATAL SECURITY

For years, a well-known British motor insurance company used to advertise its services with this wonderful line of copy:

This policy offers absolute security in the event of any kind of fatal accident.

A WINDOW PAIN

Before air conditioning made it unnecessary for motorists to drive with their windows down, accidents between vehicles in which people had their arms, even their heads, outside were not infrequent. One insurance claim, which was received after a driver had hit the proverbial brick wall, read:

I thought my window was down, but I found out it was up when I put my head through it.

A BUMP IN THE REAR

In 1948, an American motorist from Ohio tried to explain to his insurers the accident he had caused in these words:

As I approached the crossing I started towards it and crashed into Miss Miller's rear end which was sticking out into the road about a foot. Luckily she escaped injury and the damage can be easily put right with a new coat of paint.

ANOTHER PROBLEM CROSSED

Railway crossings were a common enough sight in America for many years and those without gates demanded care from drivers. The *Herrington Sun* newspaper in Kansas was responsible for this comic misprint in 1952:

The courts have held that in the case of an auto driver who neglects the utmost precaution at a railway crossing and is struck by a train, he is guilty of negligence and not entitled to recover.

A PRETTY STATE OF AFFAIRS

Explaining to his insurers how his car had ended up in a ditch and he was unable to remember much about the crash, an Irishman wrote in 1958:

Owing to the steering gear going wrong, the car ran up on the fence and capsized. The ambulance took me to Dublin Infirmary for treatment under a cosmetic.

LIGHT ON THE CAUSE

A few years after this, an employee of the Glasgow Corporation Highways Department was driving a three-ton truck when it was involved in an accident. In a report for the city's insurers, the man wrote:

I was driving along when the steering went haywire. The wheels locked and the corner of Pitlochry Drive came across and hit the truck with a lamp standard.

KEEP IT IN THE FAMILY

Arguments between husbands, wives, children and relatives have been a regular cause of accidents, according to insurers. One bizarre variation on this featured a mother-in-law, according to the claim of a Liverpool driver involved in a write-off:

I pulled away from the side of the road, glanced at my mother-in-law and headed over the embankment.

A STICKY PROBLEM

In making a report to Lincolnshire County Council in the late 1950s about the number of motoring accidents which had occurred in recent years, an insurance investigator was reported to have told the councillors:

It appears that a slippery quality in a road surface is caused by the use of tar, or of bitumen, and that the condition can be avoided by the use of bitumen, or of tar.

A HIT DOWN UNDER

An Australian driver whose small truck was struck by another car on the coastal road near Brisbane duly completed his insurance claim form and wrote:

The guy was all over the road. I had to swerve a number

of times before I hit him.

THE NATURE OF THE BEAST

When a horse belonging to a farmer in Stillwater, Oklahoma, was knocked down and killed by a car in 1960, the motorist's insurers sent the man a claim form to complete. He answered all the questions until he came to one that puzzled him: 'Disposition of the carcass.' When returned, the insurers found he had written:

Kind and gentle.

ANIMAL RESCUE

A French motorist, who came to grief as he drove along a deserted road in rural Normandy, did not have much of an excuse to offer his insurers, though they were amused by his explanation:

I was thrown from my car as it left the road. I was found in a ditch by some stray cows.

DIVINE INTERVENTION

Following a storm in Acton, London, 1968, when lightning struck a church and sent rafters crashing down, destroying the vicar's car and a number of other items, the cleric was quoted in the local press as stating:

Fortunately we're insured against Acts of God.

THE WARNING CAME TOO LATE

There was also some unconscious humour in the insurance claim of a Manchester bank manager in 1972. He concluded his report of an accident in which his car had been struck by another vehicle in a busy part of the city with this sentence:

The other car collided with mine without warning of its intentions.

BEATEN BY THE POST

The Ford Motor Company has carried out a great deal of research into motor car accidents as part of its drive to produce safer vehicles. In 1975, it was reported that the company had investigated 400 accidents and discovered that 10 per cent of these involved collisions between vehicles and lampposts. A Ford spokesman said:

This fact suggests that the country's lampposts are generally badly positioned.

FROM PILLAR TO ACCIDENT

An American housewife complained angrily to her insurance company about some pillars which divided the traffic into and out of a drive-through bank in New York. Following an accident in 1994, in which she seriously damaged her car by striking one of these pillars, she wrote:

If the pole wasn't there then I sure wouldn't have hit it!

THE BLIND DRIVING THE BLIND

In 1977, an investigation was carried out in Rome into the issue of 22 driving licences to officially listed blind persons by the *Chieti*, the Italian Road Traffic Inspectorate. A statement subsequently issued to the press stated:

The investigation has revealed that though none of the applicants were blind, all of them have been drawing pensions for that deprivation.

HEDGING HIS CLAIM

A lack of vision was blamed in another insurance excuse in the 1970s by a driver in the West Country of England. Filling in his form for extensive repairs to his family saloon, the man wrote:

As I reached an intersection, a hedge sprang up, obscuring my vision, and I did not see the other car.

MOUTH OVER MATTER

New York taxi drivers are not noted for their courtesy to other drivers, especially during rush hours. However, one cabby in Manhattan who was involved in a multiple pile-up on a hot summer's day in 1983, had a perfect excuse for his claim form:

The indirect cause of the accident was a little guy in a small car with a big mouth.

A CLOSE TRUNK CALL

A Glasgow insurance broker was amazed to receive a claim in 1985 from a local driver who said his vehicle had been damaged by *an elephant*! The form was, however, accompanied by a statement from a circus owner admitting liability to the accident which had occurred while the driver was following a procession of animals. The motorist stated:

On seeing the animals I slowed down and proceeded at a respectable distance. Then, suddenly, the elephant stopped, backed a little, and sat down on the bonnet of the car.

JUST A MATTER OF PARKING

An Essex mother of three children was faced with an embarrassing claim after wrecking the family car in 1991. Giving details of the accident and its aftermath, she added:

As I normally do, I reversed the car out of the garage to take the children to school. Unfortunately, my husband had reversed it in the night before . . .

A PROBLEM BEHIND

There was probably nothing very funny about the pain that the driver of a car on his way to see his doctor in London in 1997 was feeling. But the insurance assessor who received his claim form could hardly have restrained a smile when he read:

I was on my way to the doctor with rear-end trouble when my universal joint gave way, causing me to have an accident.

THE PHANTOM CAR

Perhaps the best motor insurance excuse of all was provided by a driver whose claim was reported by the British Vehicle Rental And Leasing Association in December 1998. The man wrote:

An invisible car came out of nowhere, struck my car, and then vanished.

9

WORKING A FLANKER

Very few people can deny ever having invented an excuse for being late for work or taking time off. 'Working a flanker' has become almost an art form and there must have been a few guilty consciences in October 1999 when a survey by Gee Publishing came up with the statistics that absence from work is reckoned to cost British business £13 billion a year – or £533 per employee. The investigation revealed that on average staff in the big companies took off twice as many days as those in businesses with less than 100 employers – 10 days as opposed to five. And if that wasn't bad enough, over 40 per cent of the firms questioned claimed that absence had increased considerably over recent years.

Of course, not every one of these workers was pulling a fast one, taking a sickie, or just trying it on. People do get stressed and ill. But skivers and those caught napping had better beware – the computer is now apparently being brought into the war against the flanker. It seems programs can now be designed to monitor trends so that people who regularly take off Mondays and Fridays can be spotted. So if the cap fits don't wear it. In this context, I'm always reminded of the comment overheard in 1984 by the Swiss businessman, Fritz Herdi, of a boss talking to one of his recalcitrant employees: 'Are you even later for work than usual today, or are you coming back from lunch unusually early?'

But despite all that bosses and technology can do, the 'great office excuse' still flourishes. They come in all shades of ingenuity, like this one reported in *The Daily Telegraph* in March 1981. The story concerned a Miss Valerie Biddoe who appeared before an industrial tribunal. She was appealing against her dismissal and was asked why she was so persistently late for work. She replied:

My boyfriend will not allow me to leave his car until I have agreed to marry him.

A LEARNING CURVE

For years, what was said to be the best excuse for lateness ever given by an employee of Gamage's Store in London was pinned up on the staff notice board. It was a verbatim account of the conversation between a departmental manager and one of his staff. The names, sadly, are not recorded:

'You've been late five times in a row!'

'Yes, sir, and you said I could never learn anything!'

NO WIN SITUATION?

The story is told at Highbury, the ground of Arsenal FC, of the office boy who was suddenly confronted by his boss in the midst of a crowd watching a midweek afternoon match in the early 1960s. The boy was looking glum as the team were already 3–0 down. In order to watch the game, he had given the excuse to his boss that he needed the time off from work to attend his uncle's funeral. When asked to explain how he came to be at a football match, the boy replied without a moment's hesitation:

Well, it will be his funeral in a minute, sir – he's the referee!

THE CHEQUE IS *STILL* IN THE POST

The classic excuse used by employees every day of the working year about the cheque being in the post has inspired many stories, true and apocryphal. In one famous case the claim was actually true – but it took half a century to prove. According to the *Daily Herald* of 23 October 1950, an unopened letter posted in Slough in 1895, containing a cheque for £38 14s 4d, had just been found by workmen while demolishing a letter box in Rocksborough Park, Harrow. The newspaper added:

The letter, addressed to a Mr W F Dauby, is believed to have been put into the box while it was freshly varnished and to have stuck to the back of it ever since.

A HAMMER BLOW

During the height of the popularity of the Dracula movies made by Hammer Films and starring Christopher Lee in the early 1960s, a columnist on the *Daily Express* quoted an excuse which he said had been made to a major London department store by one of its employees:

I shall not be coming into work today as my mother-in-law has come back as vampire. We will have to track her down to her coffin and drive a stake through her heart so that she can rest in peace. *One day off will be sufficient.*

THE SLIPPERY WORKER

The television script writer, Robert Holmes, who was a major figure in the success of the long-running serial *Doctor Who*, used to tell the story of an Irish labourer he knew who was habitually late for work but was invariably inspired to produce an excuse. In the winter of 1976, on one particularly cold morning, the man arrived over an hour late and explained to the foreman that the road had been so icy underfoot that every step he took forward had caused him to slip two paces back. But, the boss exploded, at that rate he would never have got to work at all. Came the reply:

True enough, sir – but didn't I turn round and walk the other way!

WHEN THE TIME IS RIGHT

The British satirical magazine, *Private Eye*, quoted the following excuse in May 1996. Although no source was given, the writer was said to work for a Manchester-based computer company.

I set half the clocks in my house ahead an hour and the other half back an hour on Saturday and spent 18 hours in some kind of space-time continuum reliving Sunday. I was able to exit the loop only by reversing the polarity of the power source to exactly e*log(pi) in the clocks in the house while simultaneously hitting my dog on the nose with a rolled up copy of The Times. *Accordingly, I will be in late – or early.*

A RUSH OR EXCUSES

It should come as no surprise to learn that ever since the days of President Nixon, Washington DC has been regarded as one of the great excuse centres of the world. The prestigious newspaper, *The Washington Post*, even ran a competition in August 1998 inviting readers to send in their favourite excuses for getting a day off work. The folk who live and work in the seat of American government did not disappoint, as this selection of the top twelve reveals:

- *When I got up this morning, I took two Ex-Lax in addition to my Prozac. I can't get off the lavatory, but I feel good about it.*
- *Constipation has made me a walking time bomb.*
- *If it's all the same to you, I won't be coming in to work. The voices told me to clean all the guns today.*
- *I can't come into work today because I'll be stalking my previous boss who fired me for not showing up for work. OK?*
- *I am stuck in the Blood Pressure Machine at the supermarket.*
- *I have just found out that I was switched at birth. Legally I should not come to work knowing my employee records may now contain false information.*
- *My stigmata is acting up.*
- *The psychiatrist said it was an excellent session. He even gave me this jaw restraint so I won't bite things when I am startled.*
- *The dog ate my car keys. We're going to hitch-hike to the vet.*
- *I know we have a deadline to meet but I have a rare case of 48-hour projectile leprosy.*
- *I am extremely sensitive to a rise in the interest rates.*
- *I prefer to remain an enigma.*

CAUGHT NAPPING

If you require an excuse for being caught napping at your desk, try one of these top ten provided by the *Daily Mirror* in April 2000 for its weary readers. They were drawn from a selection posted on the internet to help provide answers for that awkward moment when the boss suddenly looms into sight:

- *Well, it worked for Reagan, didn't it?*
- *I was testing the keyboard for drool resistance.*
- *That cold cure I took last night just won't wear off.*
- *Ah, the unique and unpredictable Arcadian rhythms of the workaholic.*
- *This is the 15-minute power-nap they raved about at the last management course.*
- *I'm doing the Stress Level Elimination Exercise Plan [SLEEP] I learned at the last seminar.*
- *This is in exchange for the six hours last night when I dreamed about work.*
- *It's OK, I'm still billing the client.*
- *Oh, you just interrupted me when I had almost figured out the solution to our biggest problem.*
- *I thought you had gone for the day.*

INTERNATIONAL BUNK-OFF DAY

If you haven't found the perfect excuse to get some time off work in this chapter – or even got an idea – then don't despair; 6 April each year has been declared 'World Call in Sick Day'. Boasting its own rallying call, 'Slackers Unite', a website now exists to provide advice for those after a day of leisure. I quote:

Bunking off is a delicate art. Here are some tips, sick

sound effects and that all-important random sick call excuse generator. So if you've not milked it already get online to: www.getodd.com/raz/sickday/sickday.html.

10

SEXCUSES

Two's company, an old saying goes, but three can add up to adultery: and when it comes to the eternal triangle, the excuses that some partners have offered when caught playing away from home have ranged from the ridiculous to the utterly hilarious. It's been claimed that where married men are concerned, the excuse most frequently used by them to a mistress – or, for that matter, any woman they want to get into bed – is, 'I never sleep with my wife.' On the other side of the coin, a favourite definition among the ladies for adultery is, 'The wrong man in the right place.'

But as far as telling whoppers is concerned, an American housewife, Charlotte Tyler of Memphis, probably produced the most extraordinary excuse in December 1973 after she admitted to having had sex with over 500 policemen in the mid-South area. When asked about the problem of having it away in squad cars with officers wearing gun belts, pistols, handcuffs and truncheons, Charlotte told a reporter from the *Memphis Press-Scimitar*, 'It's just something you have to get used to working around.' But why with so *many* men?

'I guess it may have something to do with my belief in law and order.'

JUST A BEGINNER

In 1933, a letter was received at Woking Magistrates Court in Surrey from local man, John Halstead, answering a summons against him for an affiliation order. His reply was read out by the clerk and duly reported in the *Woking Herald*:

I don't know whether or not I'm the father of the child, I'm only an apprentice.

THE CLASSIC POSITION

During a divorce court hearing, Styles *v* Styles, in Exeter in 1938, reported by the *Devon & Somerset News*, a wife accused her husband of constantly ridiculing her with quotations by famous people. This would happen when they were in public and on the rare occasions when they had sexual intercourse. What had been the final straw, she told the judge, was when she found her husband in bed with a girl who worked in the local library. Once again, he resorted to the classics to try and excuse his infidelity:

My dear, remember what Thomas Hardy said. 'A lover without indiscretion is no lover at all.'

SEEING IS *NOT* BELIEVING . . .

During the Second World War, adultery became almost commonplace when vast numbers of husbands and wives were separated by active service. However, solicitors who had specialised in divorce cases before the war, now found their earnings hard hit when the blackout was brought into force. This ruled that the windows of all houses must be securely covered so that no light would show through to provide targets for the German bombers flying overhead. According to a report in *The Daily Herald* in 1942, a lawyer defending a wife against a charge of adultery took advantage of this fact to inform the judge at Clerkenwell Court:

The evidence of the enquiry agent into this case should be discounted. The adultery alleged against my client cannot be proved as identification in the pitch dark is quite impossible.

SOMETHING HOT IN BED

A man named Oliver Thomas seeking a divorce from his wife in 1950 told a court in Bristol that he had come home early from work one afternoon and found the classic situation of his spouse in bed with another man. Her excuse, though, was very far from ordinary, according to a report of the case in the *Bristol Evening Post*. Thomas explained to Judge Wethered:

My wife was in her underwear and looked a little flustered. The man was sitting up in bed eating and she told me he had come for a hot lunch.

A BIT OF SHARED BONDING

The Christmas 1952 issue of *The Solicitor* reported an allegedly true story about an unnamed London stockbroker who had apparently returned home some weeks earlier and found his wife in bed with a man he had never seen before. According to the legal journal, the wife had an excuse all ready for her husband:

It's all right, dear, I've gone public.

STAMPING ON INFIDELITY

When a New York housewife, Betty Kelland, discovered that her businessman husband, Jim, was having an affair with his secretary in August 1956, she took swift and violent action, according to a report of the subsequent divorce proceedings in the *International Herald Tribune*. She hit him over the head with a rolling pin, pulled him around on the ground by his hair and kicked him several times in the testicles. Mrs Kelland burned his shirts, threw away his cuff links and destroyed his stamp collection. She also locked him out of the family home and made him sleep in his car. After listening to this catalogue of female rage, Judge Ewbank summed up:

I consider Mr Kelland's adultery infinitely worse than his wife's retaliation. However, I am prepared to grant him a decree because Mrs Kelland has not asked for one as she does not think her marriage has broken down.

THE STARRING ROLE

Infidelity and adultery have been a part of Hollywood for many years, and in 1957 a gossip column in the *Los Angeles Times* described the break-up of the marriage of yet another film executive and his wife. The couple, notorious for their infidelities, were not named, but one aspect of their separation was never mentioned during the divorce proceedings, the paper said:

One night, when they were sleeping together, the wife had

*a vivid dream that she was making love to her lover when
her husband walked in. 'My husband! My husband!' she
shouted in her sleep. Hearing the shrieks, her husband leapt
out of bed and hid in the wardrobe.*

A STORY OF BED MANNERS

Summing up in a divorce case in Birmingham in 1958,
the judge commented that Mrs Evans had a succession
of boyfriends. Each time they visited the house, he said,
she would trundle her bed into the kitchen, shut the
door, and remain there for a substantial time. According
to a report in the *Daily Mirror*, the judge continued:

*When the men left, Mrs Evans would trundle the bed back
into the bedroom and go to sleep. It must have been extremely
embarrassing to her husband. It is possible she just wanted to
sit and chat to the boyfriends and took the bed in because of
the lack of furniture.*

THE DANGERS OF FOREPLAY

Shortly after their wedding in 1960, Derek Forbes, a
Midlands scrap metal worker, introduced his new bride,
Nora, to his particular idea of foreplay – he would take
her through a couple of rounds of boxing before they got
into bed. According to a report in *The People*, Forbes,
32, was keen on boxing, but his 20-year-old wife was
not. Indeed, she had not been at all well lately. Three
weeks after the nuptials, Nora went back to her parents,
delivering this parting shot via the newspaper:

My husband doesn't want a wife, he wants a punchbag.

SOFTLY SPOKEN

Chico Marx, one of the quartet of film comedians, the Marx Brothers, was well known as a womaniser and master of excuses. The outgrown, modified Tyrolean outfit that Chico wore on the screen was very different from the stylish suits he wore when not working. On one famous occasion in 1960, reported by the show-business magazine, *Variety*, while he was appearing on Broadway in a musical, Chico was caught in a compromising situation with a chorus girl. Showing the same mastery of the ad-lib as brother Groucho, he protested:

I wasn't kissing her – I was whispering in her mouth.

THE KISS OF LIFE

A not dissimilar excuse was used in 1984, when an English couple were jailed for making love in public on a Greek holiday beach. The problem was, a report in *The Sun* said, that over 2000 other tourists watched their antics. The man said to the Greek police:

I was just giving her the kiss of life.

THE BIG KISS-OFF

Kissing and sex also made the news in a rather more unexpected context in December 1962. A report in the *Daily Mail* in the December of that year said that mistletoe was losing its magic. Demand for the romantic berry was falling off according to a London market trader, who told the newspaper that he blamed the permissive society.

It's fast disappearing, I think, now that people have sex all the year round.

PICTURESQUE CURVES

In March 1963, a French seaman, Marcel Rivien, brought a breach-of-promise suit against his girlfriend, Noelle Michael, which was so amusing that it made the front pages of many newspapers, including *Paris Match*. It was the reason *why* Rivien wanted to spurn the red-haired beauty that made the news when he revealed all in a Marseilles court:

I cannot marry a girl who has 12 tattoos on her chest.

EXCUSE IN A FLASH

Giving evidence at Hendon Court in 1965, a police officer reported that the man in the dock had followed two teenage girls along Binney Street and tapped one on the shoulder. Both had turned around, screamed and run away. The officer and a colleague then arrested the man and found that he was exposing himself. According to a report of the case in the *News of the World*, the policeman continued:

I asked the accused what he thought he was doing. He said, 'Nothing, nothing. I was just waiting for my wife.'

NIGHT OUT WITH THE GIRLS

During a particularly acrimonious divorce case in Manchester in 1967, reported by the *Manchester*

Evening News, a husband was clearly losing the argument with his wife's lawyer about his serial infidelities. Finally, while being cross-examined about being seen in the company of his latest girlfriend, a pretty young blonde, in a local night club, the man rounded on his questioner:

There was a good reason for that. My father gave me two pieces of advice when I got married. First, always insist you spend one night a week out with the boys. Second, don't waste it on the boys.

SQUEAKED ON BY A BED!

An Australian travelling salesman explained to a judge in Sydney in 1965 how he had first discovered that his wife was being unfaithful to him. His job kept him on the road from Monday to Friday, he said, and when he got home for the weekend he liked to enjoy sex with his wife. But her guilty secret came out, according to a report in the *Sydney Bulletin*, when the couple started making love one Sunday morning. The salesman explained:

As my wife and I made love, the bed springs began to squeak. Then I heard someone in the next apartment shout out, 'Can't you at least stop that racket during the weekends?'

COITUS INTERUPTUS

The art of using excuses carefully in sex cases has rarely been better demonstrated than in a hearing at Old Street Magistrates Court in London in November 1968, and reported verbatim by the *Evening Standard*:

The judge said that when the organist started to spend a lot of time at the rectory, Mr Jamal warned his wife 'not to get into a position from which it might be difficult to withdraw'.

COC AU VAN

It was the nightmare situation every illicit lover dreads. While making love to his girlfriend in the back of a small car in Regents Park, London, in July 1976, a man slipped a disc and found himself trapped in his partner. Unable to move herself – or her lover – the girl had no other alternative than to press her heel against the horn to attract attention. As luck would have it, a report of the events in *Weekend* magazine said, the sound attracted a passer-by who happened to be a doctor. He took one look at the semi-naked couple and quickly summoned an ambulance and the fire brigade. By the time the firemen arrived a crowd had gathered and the fire chief decided the only way to free the hapless couple without crippling the man was by cutting off the back of the car. Half an hour later, the job done, the poor fellow was carried off, still in great pain. The girl, now fully dressed, was comforted by an ambulanceman who said her lover would make a complete recovery. Her reply was apparently audible to everyone at the scene:

Sod him. What's worrying me is how I'll explain to my husband what's happened to his car!

A SCORING CHANCE

When summonsed to appear in court in 1976, Simon

Priam, a builder's labourer from Surrey, conducted his own defence and offered a novel excuse to the court for his amorous exploits. According to a report of the case in the *News of the World*, the defendant said:

I did not intend to sleep with Mrs Spurrell as I knew she was married to my employer. However, while we were discussing Einstein's general theory of relativity I dropped off to sleep and when I woke up she was on top of me. When her husband came into the room, I said, 'My wife thinks I am at West Ham. Do you know the score?'

THE NAKED TRUTH

The wife of a London insurance broker found herself in a tricky situation when she and her husband were invited to a party given by his boss in Neasden in the spring of 1977. She explained the sequence of events in an amusing letter signed 'Mrs X' to *Men Only* the following June:

The door of the house was opened by the boss's wife who, much to my husband's astonishment and my shock, wasn't wearing a stitch of clothing. I was embarrassed, distressed and angry, but what can you do when your husband's boss and his wife are involved? I pretended not to notice a thing.

LEARNING CURVES!

The late Dick Hills, the famous comedy scriptwriter who provided material for Tommy Cooper, Bruce Forsyth, Jimmy Tarbuck and many other top British comedians, was a great collector of excuses. He particularly enjoyed what he called, 'Excuses for Being

Found in a Compromising Situation with a Member of the Opposite Sex by your Beloved Spouse.' Dick never claimed that his six favourite examples were true – but said he was willing to reimburse anyone who claimed to be the original source:

- *A wife finds her husband in bed with town flirt.*
  'Lionel! How could you!' she says.
  He smiles. 'Just watch and learn. Watch and learn!'
- *The only time I've ever felt the seven-year-itch and you walk in!*
- *Scene in court: 'I can understand your anger at finding your wife in bed with another man, but why did you shoot her?'*
  'Well, your honour, it saves me shooting a different man each week!'
- *It only proves you're right, dear – I am over-sexed!*
- *Wife to businessman husband: 'What's going on with you and your secretary?'*
  'Not much, most of it comes off.'
- *No excuse, dear – deep down, I always thought that you preferred to watch!*

POTTING FOR PLEASURE

A London window cleaner notorious for his ways with the ladies was sued for divorce by his wife in July 1978. During the course of the hearing, reported by the *Daily Express*, it was stated that the man had been found with another woman in his bedroom with all the lights out. When asked to explain what he was doing, the window cleaner replied:

Playing snooker.

A CASE OF OVER-EXCITEMENT

When a construction engineer who had been working in Saudi Arabia for some time returned to his home in Northumberland in October 1979 and rang the door bell, he found himself in for quite a surprise, a report in the *Northumberland Gazette* said. Because, as Desmond Yeats later explained to the police, the door was opened by a completely naked man. Yeats promptly knocked the man down and then found himself being screamed at by a woman at the top of the stairs. At this he realised the lady was *not* his wife:

I suddenly remembered my wife had sold the house and gone to live in the United States. I was a bit over-excited, but I had been working in Saudi and had just had my first drink in nine years.

FRUCTIFYING BEHIND BARS

The Italian prison authorities found themselves in an embarrassing situation in April 1981 when it was revealed that a female terrorist, Francesca Bellere, serving a 16-year sentence in a maximum security prison, had become pregnant. In a specially prepared statement for the press, reprinted in the *Gazetta Del Popolo*, a spokesman for the prison service said:

This sort of thing makes nonsense of our claim that Italy's maximum security prisons are impregnable. However, we feel sure she was fructified while she was in the dock.

THE BREAST SOLUTION

Stories of wives looking for excuses not to have sex with their husbands are legion. But a Dutch housewife came up with a bizarre solution to the problem according to a report in *Medical Practice* in January 1980. The facts came to light when the wife and her husband, Huslan Dek, a banker, visited their GP, Dr Arno Hammacher, in Utrecht. At the surgery, the man complained of soreness under the arms and was asked to strip to the waist. Thereupon Dr Hammacher pointed to his very pronounced breasts and asked how long they had been there. The banker replied that he did not know and had never noticed them before. At this moment, the medical journal noted, Mrs Dek confessed:

She admitted that she had been giving him regular doses of female hormone tablets with his coffee for the last twelve years as she had a natural distaste for sexual intercourse and wished to curb his urges.

ONE BOOB IS NO EXCUSE

Another excuse about a long-time condition was revealed in March 2000, when a husband in Cairo sought a marriage annulment. The court was told that the man was making the application because he had just discovered – 20 months after the wedding – that his wife had only one breast. However, according to an account of the proceedings in *Al Mussawar*:

The man claimed he had been misled by his wife, but the court ruled that there was 'no reason why the couple could not perform their normal marital duties'.

THE UNCUT REASONS

The story of Lorena Bobbitt, the American wife who used a steak knife to cut off the penis of her philandering husband, John Wayne Bobbitt, in June 1993, is famous all over the world. Bobbitt, of course, managed to get his appendage restored and has since become something of a celebrity – claiming recently to have had sex with almost a hundred women. He also tours with a live show featuring girl dancers and 'The Penis' with its 360-degree scar. Such is the interest that David Letterman's *Late Night Talk Show* ran a competition for 'Lorena Bobbitt Excuses', inviting viewers to provide reasons for her cutting retaliation. The best half dozen of these were:

- *I was tired of playing 'Got Your Nose'.*
- *It was good practice for carving the Thanksgiving turkey.*
- *I was trying to cut the price tag off his new pyjamas when he sneezed.*
- *That's what he got for hogging the TV remote control.*
- *I fell asleep whittling in bed.*
- *What can I say? I love a good joke!*

NINE BRIDEGROOMS FOR ONE BRIDE

Labelled as 'Britain's Busiest Bride', a 29-year-old mother of two, Samantha Parry of Brixton, was jailed for nine months in November 1999 for bigamously marrying seven Nigerians in the space of 15 months. The case was heard at Kingston Crown Court where it was alleged that Samantha had been tricked into the sham weddings by a bogus solicitor who was subsequently arrested. According to a report in *The Daily Telegraph*, she told the police:

I never knew I was doing anything wrong. I know you are going to say it is far-fetched and that I am stupid and dopey but it is true. I just thought I was helping them.

THE EXCUSE-ME DANCE

In February 2000, *The Sunday Times* reported what it called 'The Brawl of the Week' when a 77-year-old man was given a suspended prison sentence for fighting at a tea dance. It was alleged that Aubrey Powell had attacked another pensioner, 71-year-old Mark Lester, with a file wrapped in a tea towel after being accused of sexually harassing dance partners at Brent Town Hall in London. Harrow Crown Court was told that the police had actually been present at a previous dance in the town hall after earlier trouble between the two men. After the hearing, Powell told reporters:

He said I was interfering with the ladies, but I'm a gentleman. And, anyway, I'm impotent.

THE ZIPPERGATE GIRL

The scandal involving US President Bill Clinton and the White House intern, Monica Lewinsky, has been blown up into more column inches than any sex story in recent years. The lady herself, now something of a celebrity as well as a spokeswoman for WeightWatchers, has delivered many memorable lines about her dalliance with Clinton, including one to the magazine *Jane* in April 2000. When asked why she did what she did, she said:

Bill is the most charismatic man. Any woman alone in a room with him for five minutes would have done the exact same thing.

11

SICK AS A PARROT

There are two favourite phrases associated with the world's number one sport, football: 'over the moon' for winning a match (no matter how) and 'sick as a parrot' when you've lost (ditto). The imagery of the first is obvious enough – but why the comparison with a member of the exotic order of birds known as the *Psittaci*, which are found in abundance in the tropics and make excellent pets? Certainly, their plumage can be just as colourful as some teams' football strips (especially away colours) and they have a talent for imitating the kind of raucous human speech often heard at football grounds. But *sick*? Parrots are actually very healthy birds, vegetarian in their diet, and can live to be over 70. Nor do they vomit – although to be strictly accurate, in moments of affection they can regurgitate little love pellets for their owners.

So why should football give currency to such a baseless slur on our feathered friends? It seems to me to have become a cliché to cover a multitude of excuses by players, managers and fans – the sort that will be found in this section. The mere mention of the phrase reminds me of a classic cartoon by Barry Fantoni, which appeared in *The Times* in January 1984 after it had been announced that General Motors were to sponsor a soccer school for young players. The picture showed a footballer being interviewed by a TV reporter and telling him: 'I'm over the radiator, Brian, and they're sick as a camshaft.'

The tradition has been perhaps most famously exemplified by Manchester United's Scottish-born manager, Sir Alex Ferguson, well known for his terse *bon mots*. In April 1996, when his all-conquering team were brought down to earth by those perennial strugglers against relegation, Southampton, in a game which the Saints could (and should) have won by more than 3–1, the boss of Old Trafford, speaking at the press conference afterwards, put the defeat down to his players' new change of *kit*. He explained.

The fellows didn't like the grey shirts. They couldn't see each other.

THE BAD LUCK OF THE DRAW

Another Scotsman, a goalkeeper, 'Jock' Martin, was one of the pioneers of this kind of excuse back in the early 1950s. Playing for Scotland in a World Cup qualifying match in Basle, Switzerland, in June 1954, the luckless Martin was on the wrong end of a thrashing by Uruguay in which his team went down by 7–0. Speaking to the world's press afterwards, Martin came up with an excuse that must have been echoed hundreds of times ever since:

We never get on so well when we're playing away from home.

BLAME THE REF!

Ralph L Finn, a famous Fleet Street football writer who covered the English soccer scene for many years, compiled a list of his favourite manager's excuses after they had been beaten, which he published in the *Sunday Dispatch* in December 1960. Although Finn did not name those responsible for the quotes, his top five were:

- *We never got a decision – the referee was against us.*
- *The sun was in our keeper's eyes all the second half.*
- *Our lads couldn't keep their feet on the wet pitch.*
- *It was the new ball, we weren't used to it.*
- *The crowd just never got off our backs.*

THE COST OF PROMOTION

The use of footballers in promoting commercial products is a multi-million-pound business today. In the 1960s, the concept was still in its infancy, when Esso used picture cards of the leading players to help sell petrol at its filling stations. The company's lead was soon followed by others, which provoked a controversy in the national press about gifts versus value, and drew from an Esso spokesman this unintentionally comic excuse reported in the *Daily Express* in 1966:

If all other petrol companies ceased giving gifts we should be the first to stop. As it is, we must reluctantly continue.

CROSSMATCH OF THE DAY

Like millions of other supporters around the world, Marinko Janevski of Zagreb enjoyed watching football.

As a policeman, he was also regularly detailed to be a crowd control officer, which meant he got a front seat at big games. Even off-duty, he liked nothing better than watching the sport on television. In 1969, however, Janevski's passion for the game landed him before a court in Zagreb charged with the murder of his wife. A report of the trail in *Narodni List* quoted his explanation:

I was watching football on television. My wife tried to stop me. I strangled her. I always get excited when watching football.

TOP SCORER

Ute Winter, the wife of the manager of Mainz FC in Germany, was sued for divorce by her husband in June 1975. The divorce court was told how Ute's husband had caught her in bed with the club's star striker. Then the goalkeeper – and next with the nifty little left-winger. This trio was then followed by the rest of the team into the lady's amorous embraces, according to a report of the court case in *The Sunday Telegraph*. In one season, Ute also allegedly slept with the whole reserve team before her long-suffering husband finally sued for divorce. Asked if she had any excuse for her behaviour, the pretty blonde wife said:

I just wanted a little tenderness.

UP THE ARSENAL

In November 1976, Tom Wattle, who described himself as a keen Chelsea supporter, was fined £10 for sticking a hot dog up the anus of a police horse, Eileen, as he was leaving a game at Stamford Bridge. A report of the case in the *Fulham Chronicle* said that Wattle told the arresting officer:

I was overcome with excitement after the match. I wanted to get rid of the hot dog and just at that moment the horse wandered by. I intended no harm and am a genuine animal lover.

THE DROPPING OF CHEESECAKE

After four seasons of failing to win a single match, the team of Greentown BME decided to drop their goalkeeper, Thomas Haycock, according to a report in the *Yorkshire Post* in November 1977. The club's manager, Harry Lash, said that although the goalkeeper weighed almost 20 stone and had let in 107 goals in three matches, it was being called 'Cheesecake' which had 'really caused his game to fall to pieces' and resulted in him being dropped. Haycock responded:

Why blame me? If the team worked together I would have nothing to do. Instead, they began to call me 'Cheesecake' when the ball was flashing around me. We were only losing 17–0 at half-time. They give up too easily.

THE LAST SHOT AT GOAL

The match between Calenzana and Murato on the island of Corsica was drawing towards a dramatic finish in a goalless draw in October 1978. After several seasons of defeats by Murato, the supporters of Calenzana were excited at the thought of denying their greatest rivals a victory. Just as the final seconds ticked away, one of the Murato forwards let loose a high, swerving shot towards their opponents' goal – according to a report in the *Sunday Express* – which seemed destined to break the deadlock. Instead, there was the sound of an explosion and the ball fell to the ground well short of the goal just as the referee's whistle blew. The sequel to the match was an appearance in court in Bastia for one of Calenzana's fans, Jean-Marie Lucchetti, who confessed to the judge:

I could not bear to see Murato win again. So I drew a revolver from my pocket, took aim at the ball, and hit it before it could enter the goal.

THE LOSER WINS

A case of loser takes all occurred in October 1980, when the Turkish football club, Orduspor, gave their keeper a £50 bonus after their match with rivals Gaziantep. Explaining the reason for this despite the fact Orduspor had lost 4–0, the club chairman told the weekly journal, *Yedigun*:

We gave him the money because we expected to lose the game by at least double figures.

SPOT THE NOSE

The 'spot-the-ball' competition has been a favourite for years with newspaper readers all over Britain. Except those in the area of Wales covered by the *Snowden Gazette*, apparently. In 1983, after receiving a number of complaints from readers, the paper's Sports Editor, David Gwillim, announced that 'spot-the-ball' was being replaced by a new competition he had designed himself. He explained:

It's very simple. We show a picture of a sheepdog trial without a sheep dog. Competitors place an X where they think the dog's nose should be.

CAUSING A STINK

The excuse which caused Burnley to cancel a third division match with Sheffield United in September 1983 did not impress the United manager, Ian Porterfield. The FA agreed to the postponement after the Burnley manager John Bond reported that 13 of his men were ill or injured. In a report in the *Daily Express*, Porterfield told one of the paper's sports writers:

I'm appalled at this. It stinks. We played Burnley Reserves last night and nobody said a thing.

THE FALL GUY

Also in September 1983, Southend FC announced that they had signed Fulham goalkeeper Gerry Peyton on a month's loan after their reserve keeper, John Keeley, had been suspended by the club for two weeks. Explaining the reason to the *Southend Times and Recorder*, a club official said:

Keeley has been suspended because he refused to come out for the second half of a reserve match against Brentford after he was criticised for letting in a goal.

DEFENSIVE ERRORS

The Botswana Defence Force football team, who toured England playing a series of friendly matches in the spring of 1984, won a lot of admirers for their style of play. On 12 May, *The Times* carried a report of their spirited victory of a London District Services side by 6–3, after which a spokesman had said:

They don't know how to defend – but they're great on the attack.

THE ULTIMATE HOOLIGAN

When Jan Giersbergen, a 20-year-old supporter of Volendam, the Dutch first division football club, was arrested at a game in October 1984, he was found to be carrying a homemade bomb. The contrivance consisted of a piece of lead piping stuffed with explosive powder. According to a report in *The Times* of the subsequent trial, Giersbergen also had on him a bicycle chain, a knife with an eight-inch blade and a knuckleduster. Before being jailed for two months, he told the court:

I just wanted to show my support for the team.

NO SPELL OF LUCK

After a string of bad results, Catania FC in Sicily decided to seek the aid of a magician in an effort to get some good luck in March 1985. However, despite the best efforts of Claudio Fisetto, the fortunes of Catania did not improve and after yet another 2–0 defeat by Fiorentina, the magician was given his cards. Fisetto complained to the *Corriere del Sport*:

They dismissed me just when I was starting the study in depth.

FROZEN TO THE SPOT

Mike Bennett, the goalkeeper of St Phillips FC of Bristol, stood rooted to the spot as a goal kick by his opposite number playing for Old Georgians sailed over his head and into the net during a game in November 1989. The goal, a few minutes from time, effectively settled the game for Old Georgians, who won 3–1. Later, Jeff Davies, the manager of St Phillips, excused his static keeper in a statement to the *Bristol Evening Post*:

He had been standing in the cold wind, rain and hail-stones so long that his lips were blue and he couldn't talk or move. We had to carry him off the pitch, give him a hot shower and send him home to bed.

RUBBING IN THE POINT

The coach of a football club in Pretoria, South Africa, was charged with indecent assault after a game in April 1990. *The Cape Town Argus* reported that Jozyk Kawalsky had denied the accusations and issued a statement in which he said:

I was expecting James Meyerspark, who had been injured in yesterday's match, to come in for a massage. I was not wearing my glasses and when Mrs Meyerspark came in I began massaging her straight away as I was expecting several other members of the team. As soon as I realised my mistake I stopped.

MISSED THE BUS

The game between London rivals Chelsea and Tottenham Hotspur at Stamford Bridge in December 1990 was delayed for ten minutes because of the visitors' lateness in arriving at the ground. Spurs faced the added indignity of losing 3–2 and being fined £20,000. It fell to their manager, Terry Venables, to explain their excuse to the press:

We stopped for lunch at the Royal Lancaster Hotel on the way to Chelsea. After the meal we discovered the team coach had been towed away for illegal parking. It even contained all our kit.

FREE TRANSFER

A prison goalkeeper was in trouble with staff and fellow inmates after deliberately letting in 15 goals in a match in Gwent in December 1994. *The Guardian* reported that Paul Morgan was annoyed at being disciplined for swearing at warders and made no effort to stop attempts on goal during Prescoed prison's 15–5 defeat at the hands of a club side, Fairfield United. The goalkeeper's actions led to an angry after-match confrontation with the other players in the back of the van that was returning them all to prison. Prescoed's prison governor, Nick Evans, told *The Guardian*:

We are an open prison and couldn't guarantee his safety. So he has been given a free transfer to another jail in Gwent.

THE RESULT OF EXTRA TIME

When the Israeli team lost 5–0 to Denmark in a European Championship game in November 1999, supporters were furious over reports that it was because the players were exhausted after an all-night party with call girls. The newspaper, *Ma'ariv*, claimed that the players partied until dawn at their hotel before the game with Denmark. But the national coach, Shlomo Scharf, offered the excuse that only wives and girlfriends were at the hotel and added:

The girlfriends of the players are very pretty and maybe the chambermaids don't know they are not escort girls.

ON THE GAME

The fans of Zambia also looked for an excuse when their team was knocked out of the African Nationals Cup by Senegal in February 2000. The supporters blamed the poor performance on prostitutes in Lusaka. According to a report in *The Sunday Times*, the fans confiscated the prostitutes' handbags before chasing them through the streets of the city. A supporter explained:

The women should have been watching the final match against Senegal instead of working. They are a source of bad luck when tournaments are taking place.

OVER THE MOON

Kevin Keegan, the current manager of England, has proved to be an expert at the quick quote and the swift excuse. After a distinguished career as a player, Joseph

Kevin Keegan – he dropped his first Christian name when he signed as a youngster for Scunthorpe – has brought a wealth of practical experience and a mastery of double-speak to all his press conferences and media broadcasts as these 12 classic examples demonstrate:

- *England have the best fans in the world and Scotland's fans are second-to-none.*
- *They're the second best team in the world and there's no higher praise than that.*
- *I know what is around the corner – I just don't know where the corner is.*
- *You can't do better than go away from home and get a draw.*
- *I'd love to be a mole on the wall in the Liverpool dressing room at half-time.*
- *Chile have three options – they could win or they could lose.*
- *Gary always weighed up his options, especially when he had no choice.*
- *It's like a toaster, the ref's shirt pocket – every time there's a tackle, up pops a yellow card.*
- *In some ways, cramp is worse than having a broken leg.*
- *The 33- or 34-year-olds will be 36 or 37 by the time their next World Cup comes around, if they're not careful.*
- *The tide is very much in our court now.*
- *England can end the Millennium as it started, as the greatest football nation in the world.*

12

A POT-POURRI OF EXCUSES

The familiar term pot-pourri, which is used to describe a fragrant container of sweet-scented materials – usually dried petals of one sort or another – comes from the French *pot* – a pot, obviously – and *pourri* which, curiously, means rotten. This last chapter of the book is a collection of plain rotten excuses. It might even be called an apologia of excuses.

Big business, in particular, is constantly striving to achieve new heights (or lows) of ingenuity when it comes to explaining to the public – and, especially, its shareholders – just *why* profits have fallen. Some of the excuses almost put British Rail's 'wrong kind of leaves' to shame. The government is a favourite, of course, as is the European Union and any sort of foreign competition. The strength (or weakness) of the pound is up there with the interest rate and a recession (when applicable), while any kind of strike and outbreaks of flu among the workforce are regular standbys. But one particular statement from the Beecham Group in the early 1970s, when it was experiencing a run of problems, is still regarded as something of a classic:

The pharmaceutical side of the business, including proprietary medicines, was clearly not helped by the very low level of winter sickness throughout the northern hemisphere.

Such sentiments deserve to be put alongside a group of other business excuses which speak of 'too much sun' (and 'too much rain'), 'the World Cup on television' and even the notorious 'self-assessment tax forms'. Let's hear the one about the weather first. It was uttered by a spokesman of Hozelock, the hosepipe and garden implements manufacturer in April 1998, blaming a fall in first-half profits on 'the wettest April of the century'. The chap explained: 'Heavy rainfall means gardeners don't need to water their gardens so they don't buy hoses.'

It seemed that Hozelock was no better off if spring proved to be very dry – because that would lead to hosepipe bans by the water companies and fewer sales of hoses, too.

The World Cup football matches shown on television in 1998 also hit the profits of several companies. Perhaps surprisingly one of these was the pub group, J D Wetherspoon – though they had banned intrusive television and canned music from their premises already – while the Rank Leisure Group, operators of the Odeon cinemas, claimed that people obviously preferred to watch football to the feature films they were showing and hence the fall in box-office takings. However, the most extraordinary slump of all was that of Kunick, who manufacture and operate slot machines. By 1998, the company controlled more than 40,000 machines and over 22 per cent was wiped off its profits while the footie was on, according to chief executive, Russell Smith, who added in a statement:

A lot of pubs brought in big screens for the tournament and, with the matches being shown in prime drinking time, people watched TV rather than play on our machines. We have never seen anything like it before.

Equally puzzled by a slump and looking for something or someone to blame were Zotefoams, a plastics firm who provide materials for toy makers. A spokesman explained: 'There has been a slow-down in supply to the three-dimensional jigsaw puzzle makers, including the four-foot-high Big Bens.'

Undoubtedly, however, the best combination of excuses offered recently came from DFS, the chain of furniture stores, who reported their first fall in profits in 28 years. What had kept customers away from their stores, Sir Graham Kirkham, the chief executive, told the press was:

High interest rates, flooding at Easter, hot weather in August, the death of Diana, Princess of Wales and the deadline for self-assessment tax forms on 31 January.

THE MOUSE THAT REARED

The world's airlines are also among the leading big business companies to come up with dire excuses, and I don't just mean the flights cancelled because of bad weather or delays due to staff shortages. Take the facts behind an incident logged as 'a delay due to conflicting traffic' when a Britannia jet was brought to a sudden halt while taxiing for take-off at Newcastle upon Tyne airport in May 1968. The 112-seater airliner, owned by the BKS Airline, was due to fly to London but was held up on the ground for some time before being allowed to commence its flight. No explanation for this was given to the passengers – an account in *The Sun* later reported – until a journalist demanded an explanation. A somewhat embarrassed spokesman for BKS admitted:

I have been in aviation for 22 years, but I have never

heard of an action like this before. The pilot said he saw a mouse run across in front of the plane and pulled up to let it pass.

A SNACK DELAY

Another bizarre delay to a flight occurred in December 1999 at Eagan Airport in Minnesota. A pilot with 22 years' service with Northwest Airlines was sacked after delaying the take-off of his flight for more than an hour. According to a report of the incident syndicated by *Associated Press*, a spokesperson of the airline explained:

The pilot did not like his meal and went off in a cab to get food.

UNABLE TO HEAR THEMSELVES SHOUT

The noise generated by aircraft taking off and landing at airports has always been a contentious issue which has regularly caused manufacturers and airlines to defend their latest planes from accusations of 'noise pollution'. In 1978, *The New Scientist* carried this statement from an aviation expert:

We take some satisfaction in the fact that the Lockheed TriStar powered by a RB211 engine, with twice the power of those in Boeing 707–type aircraft, generates no more noise at take-off than that of the population of Greater London shouting together.

A UGANDAN DISCUSSION

The only human sound that the general manager of Uganda Airlines, Adoko Mekyon, might have heard when delivering his annual report in June 1986 would have been the wails of his anguished staff at the news he was imparting. His statement was reprinted by *The Daily Telegraph*:

We are heavily overstaffed with two airworthy planes and 1100 workers. Sometimes parts of one plane are sold on the black market and bought back for the other plane. Many of the workers remain at home for weeks on end, while others have to walk 20 miles to work and are too tired to do anything when they arrive. They are not to be blamed. The money we pay is too low for lunch and dinner. Lunch, yes. Dinner, yes. But both – no. Needless to say, we are very short of passengers, too.

REST IN TRANSIT

There was considerable public anger in America in August 1987, when it was learned through the media that Interstate Airways had failed to deliver a unique package to its correct destination. A report in the *San Francisco Chronicle* explained that the package contained the bones of Private Eddie Slovak, the only American soldier to have been shot for desertion since the Civil War. The package, which had been kept since the Second World War in France where Slovak was executed, was being returned to his home town of Detroit. Instead it arrived in San Francisco, where a spokesman of the airline was asked to explain the mistake. He replied:

These things happen all the time.

WHO NEEDS PASSENGERS?

The operators of buses and coaches have had their moments, too. In 1976, the Hanley to Bagnall route in Staffordshire gained widespread notoriety because of poor service. A report in the *Staffordshire Advertiser & Chronicle* said that things had come to a head when a group of passengers using the route, led by one of the most regular users, Bill Hancock, alleged that buses on the outward journey regularly went straight past stops where queues of up to 30 people were waiting. The matter was raised with the local council, said the paper, and quoted Arthur Cholerton, the official responsible for transport, who said:

The problem is that if these buses stopped to pick up passengers they would disrupt the timetable.

BUS PASS

The man who climbed on board a bus bound for the centre of Wisconsin in America on 28 November 1999 provoked a mixture of laughter and outrage from the other passengers. For he was wearing no trousers. The bus driver refused to pull away from the stop and called the police to arrest the man. When the case came to court a few days later – an account in the *Chicago Daily News* reported – the man excused himself:

I'm sorry. I thought it was Monday.

EXCUSE OF THE DAY

Hotels and restaurants are also fine locations for the

hunter of excuses. The classic joke about the diner asking why there was a fly in his soup and being told, 'It's actually the meat, sir,' may or may not be apocryphal. But I can vouch for the story of a solicitor friend who endured a long delay while waiting for his lunch at a top London restaurant. Finally, after almost an hour, he ran out of patience and managed to catch the eye of a waiter and ask him for an explanation. Without batting an eyelid, the man replied:

I'm sorry, sir, but there are several members of staff at lunch.

BUTTERING THE CUSTOMER UP

In another London restaurant, which prided itself on its buffet table, a publisher friend was horrified to encounter a young waitress coughing and sneezing over an exposed keg of butter. He suggested, politely, that she might like to use a handkerchief while standing near the butter, to which the girl replied:

Oh, it isn't butter, sir, it's margarine.

WAKEY-WAKEY CALL

Or take the case of Newcastle businessman, Melville Summerfield, who was unexpectedly awoken at 6 a.m. by an alarm call in his room in the International Hotel, Prague. The thing was, he told *Executive Travel* in April 1986, he had not booked an alarm call and so he complained to the receptionist. Unperturbed, the girl replied:

It is the person next door to you who has booked an early

morning call. But there is no telephone in that room so would you kindly go and wake him?

DEAD TO THE WORLD

Another business traveller, Peter George, told *Executive Travel* of an even more bizarre experience he had at a hotel in New York. The story could have come straight from an episode of the madcap TV series, *Fawlty Towers*, starring John Cleese, the magazine suggested in its survey to find the best – and worst – hotels in the world. Peter George told the magazine:

When I entered my room, I found there was a corpse in the bed. I reported my discovery at the reception, but the clerk did not even look up. He simply swivelled his chair to get a new key and said, 'OK – you're now in room 208.'

ROOM FOR THE PRESIDENT

The famous American columnist, Art Buchwald, told the story – which he swore was true – of a friend who arrived at a Chicago hotel to be told that it was fully booked. For a while the man argued with the receptionist, insisting that he knew it was the hotel's policy to always keep a room or two spare for emergencies. The friend then asked, 'If the President came, you would have a room for him, wouldn't you?' The receptionist reluctantly agreed – at which Art Buchwald's friend declared:

Well, give me his room – the President isn't coming.

A SCENE STEALER

Theatres and concert halls occasionally have to resort to unlikely excuses when events overtake a performance. In September 1976, a period of prolonged drought played havoc with a production of the popular comedy, *Pyjama Tops*, while on a provincial tour, particularly when it reached the Corn Exchange in Ipswich, Suffolk. Explaining why a scene in the play was being altered, the Director of Recreation and Amenities for Ipswich Borough Council told the *East Anglian Daily Times*:

As a consequence of the present water shortage, the nude swimming scene is being removed. It will be replaced by nude badminton.

A SMILE IN TIME

The conductor who stormed off the stage at the Comic Opera in Paris in November 1978 was not suffering from a bout of artistic temperament. According to a report of the upheaval by *Paris Match*, Roberto Benzi was midway through conducting a performance of Jules Massenet's humorous opera, *Werther*, when he suddenly hurled his baton to the ground and strode from the podium. The newspaper later enquired of the maestro the reason for his sudden departure:

Because no one in the orchestra has smiled at me for over a week.

TUNING THE TRUTH

The well-known American pianist, Leopold Godowsky, combined playing concerts with teaching children to play. In an interview with *The New York Times* in 1983, he recalled being asked to instruct one totally unmusical child who was both clumsy and tone deaf. Trying his best to make something of the youngster, Godowsky side-stepped any questions from her doting parents about her progress for months on end until the day when he could make excuses no longer. Rather than face the couple, the pianist told *The Times*, he confined himself to a hand-written note, which said:

Your daughter is not without lack of talent and she manages to play the simplest of pieces with the greatest difficulty.

HARD TO SWALLOW

The reason for a riot which occurred in September 1983 at Brixton Prison in London was described as 'the flimsiest excuse ever' by the popular press. A report in the *Daily Mirror* said that 12 warders and six prisoners had to be treated in the prison hospital for their injuries after the fighting had been quelled. The newspaper added:

The fights broke out after the prisoners complained that their cans of Coca-Cola had gone flat because the warders had removed the ring-pulls because they were 'a security risk'.

LET'S BLAME THE DOG

Excuses by children have been gathered in numerous books ranging from the anonymous *Slick Excuses for Stupid Screwups*, Dan Pirarao's *The Book of Lame Excuses* and *100 Excuses For Kids* by the youthful duo of Mike Joyer and Zach Roberts who describe themselves on the back of the book as 'international authorities in the art of making excuses'. The vast majority of these excuses deal with getting the better of parents or teachers and, in many instances, are probably based on actual experience. Three favourites among my own children and their friends are:

- *Everyone else has got one.*
- *It was like that when I found it.*
- *All my friends are going.*

In Rosie Rushton's *Staying Cool Surviving School*, the author awarded the top prize for getting a day off school to the excuse, 'I felt fine at breakfast.'

And as to the little matter of homework, a group of teachers in Suffolk conducted their own poll and came up with the three most popular excuses:

- *The dog ate my homework.*
- *My homework was scribbled on by my little brother/sister.*
- *Homework tires my eyes.*

In one school, I am told, there is a teacher who keeps a list of the excuses that have been given to her over the years. This she has been known to put down in front of a pupil struggling to explain a misdemeanour, with the wry suggestion:

'Choose one of these!'

FESTIVE EXCUSES

The greetings card industry which has been making a fortune out of cards for birthdays, engagements, weddings, Christmas Day, Valentine's Day, Mother's Day and so on, has even begun introducing cards with ready-made excuses. When it comes to Christmas, though, there are still those people who believe there is no substitute for a personal notice in *The Times*. Two classic examples, both by men renowned for their humour, deserve a more permanent record:

* *Jimmy Edwards has not sent Christmas cards this year, owing to Christmas having arrived sooner than he expected.*

* *Mr and Mrs Frank Muir will not be making an announcement in* The Times *this year – instead they will be sending their friends Christmas cards.*

NETX EDITOIN PIRNTED KORRECTLY

Newspapers are prime excuse-makers when it comes to apologising for mistakes or misprints that have appeared in their pages. Here are a dozen of my favourites, beginning with a classic from the *Hartford Courant* of Connecticut, USA, which appeared in 1948 and required not one but two corrections.

For Sale. Slightly used farm wench in good condition. Very handy. Phone 336–569. A Cartwright. [March 22]

Correction. *Due to an unfortunate error, Mr Cartwright's ad last week was not clear. He has an excellent winch for sale. We trust this will put an end to jokesters who have called Mr Cartwright and greatly bothered his housekeeper, Mrs Hargreaves, who loves with him. [March 29]*

Notice! *My* winch *is not for sale. I put a sledge-hammer to it. Don't bother calling 336–569. I had the phone taken out. I am not carrying on with Mrs Hargreaves. She merely lives here. A Cartwright. [April 9]*

Another American newspaper, the *San Francisco Chronicle*, did hardly anything to ease the confusion in the minds of its readers when it ran this paragraph in 1965:

Yesterday in this column the wording appeared, '. . . fellows in the back row, among whom I was with.' That was a typographical error. It was originally written as follows: '. . . fellows in the back row, among whom I was which.' We trust that makes everything clear.

A decade later, a small rural paper in Pennsylvania, the *Titusville Herald*, took an uncompromising stand when it needed an excuse:

Just to keep the record straight, it was the famous Whistler's Mother, not Hitler's, that was exhibited at the recent meeting of Pleasantville Methodists. There is nothing to be gained in trying to explain how the error occurred.

Now for three examples from this side of the Atlantic, beginning with the *West Essex Gazette* in 1951:

In printing the name of one of the musical comedies to be presented next week as The Grill on the Train, *what our compositor meant to set was, of course,* The Girl in the Drain.

If that doesn't strike you as funny, try this excuse from the *Hertfordshire Pictorial* in 1962:

We are asked to state that Miss Butler did not stroke the cow which tossed her. It was some distance from her at first, but after she had said 'Good morning' to it, the animal rushed at her.

Finally, here is my own favourite from the *Matlock Mercury and West Derbyshire News* of September 1983:

We regret that our medical contributor is ill and therefore not able to write his weekly column, "How to be Healthy" at present.

GREAT LIES

At the dawn of the new Millennium, *The Times* ran a series of letters from its correspondents on the great lies of the previous century. Many of the lies suggested ran pretty close to being excuses and included the following classic half-dozen:

- *We must have lunch some time.*
- *I only drink red wine for the sake of my heart.*
- *I'll just have a half and then I really must be going.*
- *I only smoke ten a day.*
- *I only have television for the wildlife programmes.*
- *Oh, I never read* Hello!

MOBILE TIMES

One of the entries in the *The Times* list of great lies referred to the mobile phone which now intrudes into every part of our daily lives. The excuse for having one, it was suggested, was because, 'It's cheaper to run than you think.' Another correspondent, Adam Birchall, reported that mobiles were not quite the infallible tools they were made out to be:

Having explained to the person on the other end of the phone that I was unavoidably detained in Bristol, the guard on my train helpfully and clearly informed us over the intercom that we were just departing Dover.

Also in January 2000, a report by *The Link* revealed that according to its research into insurance claims, mobile phones were prone to bizarre accidents. The most common reason cited for losing one was leaving it on public transport or else on the roof of a car. Other excuses included dropping the mobile down a drain or a car running over it. The report added:

People also flush them down the lavatory, drop them in setting concrete and lose them out of windows when turning a corner.

DOWN WITH THE COMPUTER!

No book of excuses could be complete without at least a mention of the ubiquitous computer, as much a part of daily existence as the mobile phone. There are several lists of the favourite excuses offered by computer experts when their programs fail and the 10 most amusing posted on the Internet are these:

- *Well, it's never done that before.*
- *It's just some unlucky coincidence.*
- *It does work, but it hasn't been tested.*
- *I thought I had fixed that.*
- *Even though it doesn't work, how does it feel?*
- *Why do you want to do it that way?*
- *I can't test everything!*
- *Somebody must have changed my code!*
- *Where were you when the program blew up?*
- *Well, it worked yesterday.*

FINIS – OR, JUST ONE MORE EXCUSE

So, as we reach the last page, you might naturally wonder if there was one guaranteed, never-to-fail excuse that has come my way during the course of my research for this book. There's no way that some of them would appear here! However, you can't do much better than this:

I'm trying to see how long I can go without saying yes.